BREAK POINT

BREAK POINT

LIMITED SIGNED EDITION

Ollie Ollerton

BREAK POINT
OLLIE OLLERTON

BLINK
bringing you closer

Published by Blink Publishing
The Plaza,
535 Kings Road,
Chelsea Harbour,
London, SW10 0SZ

www.blinkpublishing.co.uk

facebook.com/blinkpublishing
twitter.com/blinkpublishing

Hardback – 978-1-788702-06-5
Trade Paperback – 978-1-788702-07-2
Ebook – 978-1-788702-08-9

A CIP catalogue of this book is available from the British Library.

Designed and set by seagulls.net
Printed and bound by Great Britain by Clays Ltd, Elcograf S.p.A

1 3 5 7 9 10 8 6 4 2

Blink Publishing is an imprint of Bonnier Books UK
www.bonnierbooks.co.uk

This book is dedicated to my mum,
whose unconditional love and care held
firm even when all around her was falling apart.

To my amazing girlfriend Laura, who will never quite
understand just how much she helps me grow.

And to my son Luke, who I missed
every day and never forgot.

Names, locations, procedures and specific events
have been redacted to protect the security of those
involved and the practices of the British Special Forces.
Everything else has been described as it happened.

CONTENTS

CONTENTS

PROLOGUE

There was not much to see on the road from Amman to Baghdad. There was sun, of course, searing a mighty hole through acre after acre of blue. Camels and goats, foraging for unseen greenery. The odd bomb crater and chewed-up vehicle, including a bright red Ferrari, which would have made more sense on the moon. And mile after mile of highway, hugged by a watery haze and cutting a swathe through the flat and featureless desert landscape.

We'd been on the road for what seemed like forever when it was my turn to take the wheel. I'd travelled 14 hours the day before and was driving on autopilot, my mind and body merged with the vehicle and tarmac beneath it. Before I'd set off that day, I'd been convinced – hopeful, even – that something big might break the monotony. But as the milometer ticked over, all I could think about was getting home and collapsing in my pit.

It was as I was telling my colleague Dave of my evening's plans that something caught my eye in my wing mirror. I looked over my shoulder to see headlights flashing behind us. It was about 17:45 and there were no other vehicles on the road. My immediate thought was that it was the American military. No problem. But as the vehicle gathered speed and drew closer, I realised that it couldn't be the Americans, because the vehicle – a black Mercedes – had blacked-out windows. I then thought it might be a security company. But if it was, what did they want me to do? Pull over? There was no way I was taking that risk.

I informed Dave that we had a possible target to the rear. Dave informed me that there were in fact two pursuing vehicles. As I was considering the possibilities, the windows came down on the front vehicle and four AK47s emerged. Oh, fuck. I glanced to my left and saw a sign that said 'FALLUJAH', and it dawned on me: that something big that I thought might happen – that I'd desperately wanted to happen – was happening, in the very place I'd imagined. 'Talk about tempting fate,' I thought to myself. 'You fucking idiot...'

My body began to roast from the toes upwards. My senses heightened, which happens when you are suddenly pitched into blackness. My mind contracted into a tangled ball of confusion so that I couldn't think. I'd gone into shock. It was as if I'd died for a second and was looking down on myself. I had no idea what I was going to do. I felt very alone, vulnerable and pathetic. An image flashed through my mind: me on the side of the road, minus my head. But it wasn't just me who was in danger of being killed, I was responsible for Dave behind me and 12 civilians piled into vans in front, employees of ABC News.

The pressure and anxiety were about to spill over when gunfire rang out. AK47 fire is very distinct and very intimidating. When there are four going off at the same time, it's like some hellish orchestra, extremely noisy and extremely nasty. In fact, and rather appropriately, it sounds like the cracking that signals the start of an avalanche. But when a couple of rounds came over the top of our vehicle, which might have buried some people, it was as if a hypnotist had clicked his fingers, bringing me out of my trance. In the military, as soon as it gets noisy, it gets real. It was at that moment that my training kicked in.

I knew that unless I tamed the stress, we were all going to die. So I gained control of my breathing, stripped away all the shit that didn't matter, and began to think rationally. The people in the vehicles in front didn't matter, it was my actions that mattered, because it was my actions that would affect them. I had to put aside all the different pressures and anxieties and deal with the threat. That was the only way to resolve the issue at hand.

It had all happened so fast, but once I had my breathing under control, everything slowed down. In effect, I was able to control the speed of events. Some might think a second is simply a second, end of story. But a second is only as short or long as the person who experiences it. You can decide how long a second is, but only if you're at ease with the situation you're in. If you're stressed and panicking, a second will feel like no time at all. If you're not, it can feel two or three times as long. You only have to watch sport to realise this. Most people facing a punch thrown by a professional boxer would wear it and hit the deck. But another professional boxer might see that punch coming, slip it and come back with one of his own. That's what I had to do.

I gave Dave the order to stand by and flung our vehicle towards the middle lane to our right. It wasn't a move I thought about, it was just instinct. The enemy pulled up beside us on our left, which was quite foolish of them: they were now boxed in by the central reservation and had no idea who we were or whether we had weapons. As it happened, I had my left hand on the steering wheel and my right hand on my MP5 kurz, which was on my lap. Meanwhile, Dave was sitting behind me with an AK47 of his own.

I checked the safety catch on my weapon was off and looked to my left through the closed window. I'd been in gunfights before, but this was the first time I'd seen the whites of the enemy's eyes. I was no more than two feet away from the guy in the passenger seat. I could have reached out and touched him. He was just a boy, wearing an Arab headdress and white robes. 'This kid is the same as me,' I thought, 'just working for someone else.' His expression wasn't aggressive or menacing, he looked like he didn't want to be there.

As uncomfortable as the boy looked, he still did what he thought he had to do. His AK47 fell in line with my head, as did the AK47 behind him. I stared even more intently into the boy's piercing blue eyes, as if trying to make a telepathic connection. I desperately wanted to hear him say, 'Don't worry, I'm not going to shoot you.' Instead, silence. I really didn't want to do what I needed to do. But all he had to do was feather the trigger and that would have been it. I had to take action. I was at break point. If I took the situation to the next level – poked the hornets' nest – it might make things worse. But it was my only hope to make things better. If I did nothing, we were going to get shot and people might die. Including me.

* * *

Stacked up against the door, balaclavas on, weapons at the ready. Who exactly is behind that door is anyone's guess. There is nothing but silence. But when we go in, it might get very noisy very quickly. People might get shot. People might go down. People might end up dead.

Contrary to what some people believe, Special Forces soldiers aren't supermen. We're just ordinary people. We can't see through walls or round corners. Bullets don't bounce off us and we don't hit the target with every shot. But, because no plan survives first contact, what we do is train and plan meticulously, so that we're battle-ready. If the shit hits the fan, we're ready to rock. Or at least we should be.

In computing, a 'break point' is defined as 'an intentional stopping or pausing place in a program, put in for debugging purposes'. In the Special Forces, we're so highly trained that we know when a break point is approaching and that we need to pause and 'debug'. That's when we take a couple of deep breaths to lower the cortisol levels, which in turn gives us greater focus. We call that recalibration. Then we do our thing. In fact, that's a Special Forces mantra: Breathe. Recalibrate. Deliver. It's our way of regaining control of a situation that might be spiralling off in a dangerous direction.

But break points aren't exclusive to soldiers in the Special Forces, they're in all of us. Our lives are dictated by break points, every day is full of them. They don't have to happen in dramatic circumstances, while you're dressed head to toe in black, wielding a laser-sighted machine gun and climbing up the side of a ship. A break point might be a crisis that needs solving in the office, an unexpected bill that needs paying or a relationship that's taken a turn for the worse. It can be even more mundane than that. A break point might be a sink full of dishes and having to decide whether to wash them before you go to bed, so that you're not faced with a kitchen full of clutter in the morning and are ready to go again. A break point might be spending the evening working on your business plan, instead of getting shitfaced down the pub. Break points are about going the extra mile, clambering over obstacles – even while travelling in what seems like the wrong direction – and facing down negatives to achieve your ambitions.

A break point is a moment you decide nothing will stand between you and your goal; a moment you decide to step out of your comfort zone in order to move forward and grow as a person; a moment you refuse to accept your self-imposed limits and go beyond what you thought you were capable of. As such, break points are more mental than physical. It might seem strange to describe coming under attack in Fallujah as being in one's comfort zone. But more comfortable than trying to fight our attackers off would have been accepting my fate and waiting to die. I knew I had to make a decision that might make our attackers even more dangerous than they already were. But it was the only way I was going to escape the situation.

Some people think that being comfortable is a good thing, but that isn't necessarily the case. Someone might feel comfortable working in an office Monday to Friday; taking home a comfortable wage; living in a comfortable house; driving a comfortable car; going on comfortable holidays twice a year. But comfort isn't normally conducive to growth and contentment. Despite your comfortable existence, you might be dying inside.

The problem is that the alternative can seem terrifying. Like making the decision to hit your attackers before they hit you. It usually means rejecting your comfortable existence and voluntarily entering a scary world of uncertainty; a world that is, on the face of it, worse than the one you're already in. But by daring to step out of your comfort zone, you might be creating opportunities to make life better.

1

MAVERICK MARINE

Being told you can't do something can be incredibly empowering, often even more so than having everything laid out for you on a plate. So I should probably thank my old maths teacher for being so negative. I was 14 at the time, chatting away in class as usual, and the teacher – not for the first time – let me have it: 'Ollerton! Pay attention!'

I sprung to my feet, like a Jack released from a box.

'I don't give a fuck about this! I'm joining the Marines!'

The teacher sneered at me from behind his desk. 'Ollerton, you'll never be in the Marines. You've got no discipline.'

That was a turning point. Almost an epiphany. It was the moment I realised that school and academia wasn't for me. And never would be. The teachers all said that I was intelligent, but I had no interest in studying. I had no interest in being part of an out-of-date system that was all about churning out little glove puppets for society: people who worked behind desks in offices, people who had expensive weddings, big mortgages and lots of debt.

The education system didn't suit me, like it doesn't suit a lot of people. I didn't want to be programmed like the other kids, have all the creativity and dreams drummed out of me. That was something I wasn't willing to accept. I was a rebel. I couldn't be doing with people telling me to do things I didn't want to do.

People who don't conform are treated with suspicion. If you're not interested in what they put in front of you at school, you're written off as a nuisance and you end up ignored and ostracised. Society isn't concerned with how well you perform as an individual, it's concerned with how well you fit into the system. But I've always believed that if you want to fulfil your potential, don't conform.

My maths teacher thought that because I refused to conform at school, it would be impossible for me to conform in the military. He thought that because I didn't have the discipline for school-work, I didn't have the discipline for soldiering. What he failed to see was that I simply wasn't interested or stimulated by what he was trying to teach me.

While teachers and schoolmates thought I was losing it, in fact it was around that time that I started to find my way. True, I was flunking exams and bunking off school, phoning up and pretending to be my mum in a ridiculous high-pitched voice: 'Matthew is ill today and won't be coming in…' (It never occurred to me to try to impersonate my dad instead, although my voice was probably closer to my mum's anyway.) But I had woken up. I wasn't a lost cause at all. For all my troubles, I was in a privileged position. I was that rare kid who knew exactly what he wanted to do with his life. There was no point flogging a dead horse, because I could already visualise where I wanted to be in a few years' time. All I cared about was becoming a soldier. I was there in spirit. I could already see myself dressed in green with a gun over my shoulder.

That wasn't the only time that someone in authority wrote me off as a kid. I can vividly remember going to the Royal Navy Marines careers office with my mum and saying I wanted to join. The woman behind the desk replied, 'If you get into the Royal Marines, what do you want to do?'

I'd studied the brochure in detail. I knew every word and every picture. So immediately after she said that, I flipped to the middle pages, where there was a photo of a combat swimmer inside a submersible insertion craft. I pointed to it and said, 'That's what I want to do.'

The careers officer looked at me and laughed. 'Everyone wants to do that. What do you really want to do?'

'That's what I really want to do.'

'Fine. Well, good luck with that...'

She could have said, 'Wow, what a great ambition. If you work hard, you'll do it.' Instead, she laughed in my face. That's the military for you, every bit as suspicious of non-conformists as the education system.

But it's probably the best thing she could have done. It's not as if I walked out of that meeting thinking, 'I'll fucking show you.' But a seed had been sown in my subconscious. That photo of the combat swimmer in his submersible insertion craft was a symbol of what I might be able to achieve if I refused to accept the limits imposed on me by others.

* * *

I loved my country and the idea of being part of a tight-knit family – a brotherhood. Since the age of 14, I'd been living it every day. Everything I watched and everything I read was to do with the military. I'd flick through *Combat Survival* magazine and daydream about being in battle and fighting an enemy. Getting in seemed inevitable. Had I not, it would have killed me.

My grandfather had been a captain in the Royal Engineers and I'd been captivated by the Falklands War as a kid, especially the TV images of soldiers returning as conquering heroes, to the sound of cheers and the sight of a thousand Union Jacks being waved. That was the last of the proper land wars, and the last Britain fought alone. When you're a boy, you only see the glamour and manliness of war, which is what gives you the passion to want to join up. You're not privy to the bits in between, the horrific realities that lead to broken minds and bodies and hundreds of shattered lives all over the country.

Someone else who unwittingly motivated me to join the military was a guy called John. He was from my home town and there was a lot of friction between us, in part because I got off with his girlfriend. It was him who made me investigate joining the Royal Marines, because he'd become this bigwig around town since joining up himself. Whenever he came back from training, he and his mates would turn up at the appropriately named Clowns nightclub and there would be a big shout out from the DJ: 'Welcome home to John, our resident Royal Marine!' I'd be leaning against the bar thinking, 'What a cock.' But I was more jealous than anything.

John found out that I was talking about joining the Marines and started telling everyone in Burton that he'd be on the training team and he'd never let me pass. Once again, it was someone telling me that I was going to fail.

I was 18 when I went on the Potential Royal Marines Course (PRMC). That was two years after I'd wanted to join up, for reasons I'll explain later. I was fit as a flea, smashed the three-day course out of the water and was accepted on 29 May 1989, a date that is etched on my mind.

I was still suspicious of authority, which some people will find strange. You can't question authority at all in the military and we're led to believe that soldiers don't last if they don't conform. But failing to conform would be a recurring feature of my military career. Even before I joined up, I was taking little jabs at the bosses.

Before leaving for the 32 weeks of basic training, I went and got my head shaved. It had to be done, but I was going to do it in my own time, rather than have it done for me. Far less cool was what happened the night before I left, when I dived off the Trent Bridge and hit the bottom of the river, bashing up my face.

On the train down to the Commando Training Centre at Lympstone, I bumped into Troy Robson, a black guy with an Afro and a big silver chain with his name on it. We ended up in 576 Troop together and formed a close bond. I loved him to bits, as did everyone else, but being the only black guy meant he was always going to get a fair bit of ribbing. One of the first things we did on arrival was pick up our gun. I couldn't wait. When I walked out of that room with my SA80 assault rifle, I was proud as anything. Standing in line, I felt like a real soldier already. Then I heard uproarious laughter, followed by the sight of Troy walking out of the room with a spear. Troy found it funny as well, but if that happened today, there would be an inquiry and sackings.

Training was brutal from the outset, as it has to be. Some recruits didn't even make it through the first night. The discomfort of being away from home and the intimidation of the training team was too much to bear. The people constantly barking at us were fully fledged Royal Marine Commandoes – gods in most of the recruits' eyes – and they scared us shitless. Not that they threw us straight into the rough stuff. The first lessons we learned were basic administration and personal hygiene, including shaving, showering and ironing. I regretted not offering to help my mum press those piles of shirts on a Sunday afternoon; I would have picked up some valuable lessons.

I was taken aback by the meticulous attention to detail that was demanded of us. At times, it seemed pointless. I hadn't joined the Marines to iron shirts. But eventually I understood that all that shaving, ironing and polishing was essentially a metaphor for operating in a warzone: sloppiness becomes habitual, and your life and your mates' lives are dependent on the minutest of details, be it the cleaning of a weapon or checking behind a door during an assault on a building.

The learning curve was steep, with each new skill taught against the backdrop of beastings so savage that no Royal Marine ever forgets them. I certainly didn't find it easy. No one does. But my passion and drive were just so strong that I knew I'd still be standing after 32 weeks, proud as punch in my green beret. My progress was made that bit smoother by my new buddies. Every Marine thinks their training troop is special. But 576 Troop contained some particularly fine people, none of whom I'll ever forget and many of whom I'm still in contact with.

In order to become a Marine, you have to pass the Commando tests. One of the tests is tackling an assault course while carrying full kit and a weapon. And the last part of the assault course is a six-foot wall. For most recruits, that's not an issue. But for the smaller guys, it can be. We had a guy we called Yoda, because he was short and stout, and he failed to get over the wall twice, which meant he had one final attempt. And we couldn't have Yoda not passing out of training with us – he was such a great bloke and a fine soldier, who just happened to be a bit shorter than the rest of us. So, Troy and I came up with a plan to get Yoda over the wall by banging a nail into the bottom of it, so that Yoda could push off it with his foot.

We managed to find a nail but not a hammer to bang it in with, so had to make do with a frying pan instead. The night before the test, Troy and I crept down to the assault course on the bottom field, which was just across from a gate manned by a sentry. Luckily, it was a stormy night, so every time there was a clap of thunder, I whacked the nail with the frying pan. It was like that scene from *The Shawshank Redemption*, when Andy Dufresne is smashing a rock against the inside of the sewer pipe. My whole body shook from the impact and the noise was terrible. Every time I hit the nail, the sentry came running out and we hit the deck. But after about ten whacks with the frying pan, the nail was finally in.

The next morning, we said to Yoda, 'Mate, when you get to the wall, look down: three bricks up, there's a little something to assist you.' We all went down to support the boys, and sure enough, when Yoda got to the wall, he bounced straight over it, like a gymnast off a springboard. The instructors couldn't believe it. And everyone else who had been struggling did the same. We never got rumbled, Yoda passed and ended up becoming a major. A couple of years ago, I found out that he now runs a climbing wall in Bristol.

As training progressed, I grew both physically and mentally stronger. In fact, I very nearly broke the camp record for the Commando test's endurance course, missing it by seconds. I was also handed my first leadership role as a section commander. That was quite a thing for someone so young and it was awesome for my confidence.

I'd just picked up my section commander tabs when I bumped into John from my home town, who looked uncharacteristically sheepish. I said to him, 'What are you doing here? I thought you'd passed?'

John looked like he wanted the ground to swallow him up. 'Erm, I'm in Hunter Troop,' he said.

At that time, Hunter Troop consisted of all the people who got injured and rarely made it through. So I was absolutely over the moon. This bloke had told everyone he'd passed and was going to be on my training team, and it turned out he had been back-squaded and was on his way out. Obviously, being the mature person I was, I told everyone who cared to listen, and made sure the whole of Burton knew about it. Exaggerating your experience in the military (known as 'bloating') never goes down very well. John never did pass, and I doubt the fact that he inadvertently helped me on my way was of much consolation.

Seeing my parents at my pass out at Lympstone was one of my proudest moments. Standing there in my Royal Marines parade dress, the peaked cap and so-called 'Blues', made me feel so powerful. I felt like a medieval knight in his suit of armour. Before that moment, I'd been a bundle of trouble, causing people bother, failing at school, never giving anything back. But now I felt like I was giving back in a big way.

Mum loved the idea of me going into the military. When she was younger, she had been accepted as an officer in the Royal Navy, but Dad didn't want her to join. She's always regretted it, so I suspect that me going in was feeding that passion. She was also relieved, because only a few years earlier, she'd been dealing with a kid who was off the rails. I could tell that my dad was proud as well, but as far as I was concerned, that day was mostly about my mum, who had sacrificed so much in bringing me up.

After passing out, I went up to 45 Commando in Scotland, which was renowned as the Arctic warfare unit. It had a reputation for being the hardest, and that's exactly what I wanted to experience. What a mistake. I should have gone down to 40 Commando in Taunton. While my lot were nicknamed the 'Arctic Warriors', the lads down there were nicknamed the 'Sunshine Boys'.

When I turned up in Scotland, I thought I was joining up with the best of the best, the absolute cream. I was incredibly keen and naïve. On arrival, I dumped my bag in the guard room, had some dinner and was escorted to my accommodation. When I opened my bag, I found a piece of paper sitting on top of my clothes. On it, someone had drawn a big cock and balls, and written, 'Welcome to 45, new boy knobber'. I thought, 'What the hell have I done?' It was someone telling me not to get too big for my boots, to stay in my box. I thought it was quite funny, but I realised that there was probably more to come.

There were a lot of beatings going on, usually after a night on the piss. I was aware that the new boys got the beats, it was just a case of when. My initiation came when I returned from the pub early, fell asleep and a guy called Ray jumped on top of me and planted his knee in my face, smashing my nose to pieces. I was supposed to be going on my first exercise to Holland the next day but ended up in hospital instead. This had been my dream, my passion, and this was my first taste of it. I expected some sort of initiation, even a bit of rough stuff, but what I couldn't understand was why this idiot had done what he'd done when he'd only recently passed out himself. Oh well, welcome to the Royal Marines...

What the commanding officers thought was going on and what was actually going on were two different things. Because Marines are extremists by their very nature, there was all kinds of ridiculous shit happening that made rugby club antics look tame. The new boys would have to drink a 'death wet', which was a pint of the top shelf of spirits, all mixed together and downed in one. That can kill people. Another time, we were drinking in town and one of the older guys tried to set me up with this girl. She wasn't really my cup of tea, but this guy kept egging me on, telling me to chat her up and take her home. Despite the copious amounts of drink, I managed to resist. The next morning, this guy said to me, 'Good job you never went with her, she's got HIV!' I thought it was a joke. It wasn't. It turned out her nickname was 'Mary the Marine Tester from 45'. The humour was just so very dark, sadistic and raw.

If you didn't go along with the initiations, the banter and the dangerous drinking, you didn't fit in. And if you didn't fit in, you might find yourself being relentlessly picked on. It was par for the course, the natural thing to do, to the extent that even people who were actually quite nice ended up being bullies, just to be accepted. The Falklands War had happened in 1982, eight years before I joined the Marines, but it wasn't usually the guys who fought there who dished this stuff out, it was mostly the guys who joined later. Maybe it was simply because they were younger, maybe it was down to the frustration at missing out on war.

Making people do stupid things after a few drinks, singing songs and wearing daft clothes is fine. In fact, there is a long-standing tradition in the Royal Marines of dressing up as women. Legend has it that every Marine has a suitcase under his bed full of beautiful dresses that even their mums would be jealous of, as well as stockings, suspenders, wigs and nail varnish. The attention to detail is meticulous. Even I got involved once or twice and looked absolutely knockout. (I once went to a fancy-dress day at school as a fairy, so it was second nature.) That sort of stuff is pretty out there, but it's harmless fun.

When I'd been in for a few months and was considered to be a bit of an old sweat, by rights it was my turn to dish out some beats. Instead, I sent one of the new boys – Tim McAllister, who would later be best man at my wedding – out to hire a sunbed. That was a slightly nicer initiation than getting the shit beaten out of him. The whole dorm ended up with nice tans and we even made a few quid out of it, because we'd charge lads from other dorms to come and use it. What that story also tells you is that I always possessed a modicum of business acumen.

Beating people up and pissing on them while they are asleep, to humiliate and demoralise them, isn't harmless fun at all. It's outright bullying, and I hated it. In case you were wondering, Ray, the guy who smashed my nose, didn't end up being a mate, he ended up getting done for manslaughter.

I joined the Royal Marines out of a deep passion to serve my country and test myself to the limit. This was an organisation I had idolised since I was a kid. So, seeing blokes who were supposed to be on my side doing things like that made me feel discouraged and a bit disappointed. How could I have admiration and respect for these people? They probably would have characterised their bullying as 'character-building'. But it was horrible, knowing that every night your door could be bust open and people could rush in and start dishing out beats. I'd known that fear before. It didn't exactly stoke my enthusiasm. Instead, it chipped away at my faith.

2

WILD CHILD

T hrough an opening in the canvas, I could see a beautiful circle of sunlit grass, closed off by lorries and neighbouring tents. In the centre of the clearing, something was moving, although viewed from the darkness of the shelter, it was nothing more than a black smudge, its edges blurred by the searing sun.

As if in a trance, I left the safety of the canopy and crept squinting into the light. The sky was an unbroken swathe of blue and the heat made my skin prickle. I blinked away the sun spots, the edges sharpened, and soon the black smudge took shape: it was a baby chimpanzee, quietly hoo-hooing to himself, between mouthfuls of assorted fruit that lay scattered around his feet. At that moment, my whole world was made up of me and that baby chimp. It was a little bit of heaven and nothing else mattered.

I held my breath and ventured closer. My mouth was dry and my heart felt like it might burst through my chest. But excitement overrode apprehension. I stood over my new friend who looked straight up at me. He had beautiful, big brown eyes and looked so innocent and vulnerable. We stared into each other's eyes for what seemed like an eternity. It was as if we had become locked together by some strange, animal magnetism. I finally remembered to breathe.

The chimp looked away, breaking the connection, and sniffed at the grass, before picking up a piece of fruit and passing it to me. It was a thrilling moment. Here I was, hanging out with a wild animal. I'd entered David Attenborough territory, the stuff of dreams. I took the fruit, pretended to eat it but threw it over my shoulder instead. The chimp didn't seem to mind. He hoo-hooed contentedly, while I beamed back at him. I'd never been so happy. I felt like I could cry.

The serenity was broken by what sounded like a fighter jet tearing through the sky. Even now, when I recall that shriek, it makes me want to clamp my hands over my ears. My eyes were drawn to a shape shuffling under a lorry, the shadow it cast becoming suddenly bigger and smaller as it went about its business. Before I could hazard a guess at what it might be, it had shot from the shadows and into the clearing. It was another chimp, but ten times as big as my new best buddy. And evidently far less friendly. The ambush was on.

The big chimp ploughed towards me in a sideways gallop, her enormous arms crashing into the turf and her legs swinging seamlessly behind them. Her shrieking became louder and louder, as if she was trying to bury me in sound. Soon, she was so close I could see her enormous teeth, unsheathed for battle. Seconds earlier, I had been bathing in bliss. Now, I was in a state of terror.

My animal instinct kicked in and I contemplated escaping. But when you're faced with a 50-kilogram ape, you can't contemplate for long. The big chimp came around the back of her little friend, as if measuring the distance, and when it had got to within about 20 feet of me, decided to pounce. What had been a beautiful bright blue was suddenly black – and getting blacker fast. It was as if the sky had collapsed and was falling in on me.

The big chimp landed right on top of me and pinned me to the floor, like a cartoon boulder. She swung her thick arms above her head and brought them down with great force onto my chest and face, like a drummer in a rock band attacking her kit. She buried her face in mine, gnashed her teeth and swivelled her neck from side to side, like a dog with a rag doll. I covered my head with my hands, but when I opened my eyes and looked through my fingers, I saw that those teeth were dripping with blood. I could feel no pain, but I instinctively knew it was my blood, not the chimp's.

It was at that moment – the most horrendous moment of my life – that pure, blind panic was replaced by the urge to live. I realised I had a choice: either I stayed on my back and let this ape beat me into an early grave, or I attempted to escape. In other words, I had to make the situation worse in order to make it better.

The baby chimp was chained to a peg, so I hoped beyond hope that my attacker was as well. I somehow managed to twist my body, which knocked my attacker off balance and created a little bit of space between us. I brought my foot up and smashed it into the chimp's chest, before scrambling back a couple of feet. The chimp regained her footing and came hurtling towards me again. But just as she was about to come crashing down on top of me for a second time, the chain that was indeed attached to her collar went taut. The chimp had lost none of her ferocity. Her shrieking was as loud and horrific as ever. Blood was everywhere, and I had no idea what part of my body it was spurting from. But I was out of harm's way, albeit by a matter of inches.

You might be wondering where I was serving when this incident took place. After all, chimpanzees are pretty thin on the ground in the Middle East. The truth is, I was only ten years old and the chimps were part of a circus visiting Burton-on-Trent. Which goes to show, your most pivotal moments – those moments that change the course of your life – can last for seconds, spring from the most unlikely of situations and be almost impossibly surreal.

My soul has been laid bare in Special Forces Selection; I've raided boats laden with drugs and hardened criminals, out at sea and under the cover of darkness; I've had machine guns pointed in my face and been under siege. But none of that came close to dicing with death with that angry circus ape. That snap decision to escape – a decision that was instinctive, that I was barely aware I was making – was what kept me alive. That was my first break point.

* * *

I don't remember much about being a kid. My childhood was a series of traumatic events that hung like enormous dark clouds over any of the good stuff. What I do know is that I was always a black sheep.

My earliest memory is being at a very posh private prep school called St Wystan's in the Derbyshire village of Repton. One day, I almost strangled a kid called Toby, who was my best friend at the time. I must have been about five and I think we were just messing around. But it was a sign of the trouble to come.

My father had an engineering business in Repton and the fact that me and my brother and sister all went to private prep school suggests it was successful. But I feel like my childhood was stolen from me. My father was very Victorian and very disciplined. He was never an affectionate man, although I don't blame him for that, that was just the norm for fathers in those days. But he was also a workhorse and he expected us to work as hard as he did. We weren't allowed to be normal kids, like our friends were. When other kids were out playing, my father would have us helping out with all kinds of stuff, whether it was building walls, sawing wood, mowing lawns or taking the dogs for marathon walks. We had a big house, with loads of land and lots of really steep banks. Once a month, my brother and I would go out and cut the lawns with a

Flymo attached to a piece of rope, lowering it down the banks and pulling it back up again. Once we'd done that, we'd chop a load of firewood. Then we'd get on our bikes, cycle to my grandad's house about six miles away to cut the grass in his orchard, before cycling home again. That was a normal weekend. At times it felt like I was my dad's employee rather than his son.

My dad was always extremely generous at Christmas. That was his way of showing love. But that didn't stop him buying us some pretty weird presents. One year, there were two presents under the tree, for me and my brother, and you could tell by the shape that they were the same thing. When we unwrapped them, we saw that they were axes. I was only about 12. We said to each other, 'Why has Dad got us axes? We're a bit old to be playing cowboys and Indians.' Two days later, we were out chopping down trees for him. The house was enormous and had stables, although we didn't have horses. Instead, the stables were filled with kindling and logs for the winter, and my dad would have us chopping that wood all weekend.

One weekend, one of my mates was supposed to come round the house but never turned up. At school the following Monday, I said to him, 'What happened to you?'

'Mate, I came round and your dad had me chopping wood for about two hours. When he decided I was finished, he told me you weren't coming out anyway.'

My dad hadn't even told me he had been there. A story like that gets around a school pretty fast. Soon, nobody was coming to visit.

While I don't remember having a lot of fun growing up, I was always a risk-taker and getting into trouble. On a holiday in Lyme Regis, I went off for a walk with my brother and sister and just when my mum and dad were beginning to wonder where we'd got to, they heard this commotion coming from the harbour wall. They wandered over to see what was going on and found me launching myself off the wall and into the sea, while crowds of older kids stood around cheering. I was only three years old. Another year in Lyme Regis, a big fishing hook went through the top of my leg. But because it was my favourite hook, the only thing I cared about was that they'd have to cut it off. And there was the time in France when I dropped a couple of bottles of lemonade in a shop and they exploded onto my legs. When I returned to the caravan, my legs were caked in blood and my poor mum was hysterical.

When I was about seven, I watched a *Tom and Jerry* cartoon in which Jerry electrocuted Tom and you could see all his bones lit up inside him. I thought that looked brilliant and wondered if it would work in real life. So I went upstairs to my bedroom, took the bulb out of my bedside lamp and stuck my thumb in the socket. The lights all over the house started flickering and my mum could hear me from downstairs, going off like a car alarm. When she burst into my bedroom, my hair was standing up on end and smoking, as was my thumb. I've still got a lump on my thumb from that incident today.

There was also the time my brother and sister locked me in a suitcase and stuffed me in a cupboard. I managed to escape, fell out of the cupboard and landed on top of a Tonka toy, splitting my nose open. Oh, and I almost forgot: I was run over twice. The first time I was on my roller skates, went between two parked cars and got hit by a Granada, dislocating my shoulder and trapping all the nerves. I could have lost my arm, because the blood supply was cut off. The second time, I was on my BMX, showing off in front of some girls. I almost feel sorry for that chimp: there she was, minding her own business on her afternoon off, and then a mentalist like me came wandering into her life.

I'd be the kid who went hunting through the house for Christmas presents. My brother and sister, who are both older than me, would say, 'What are you doing that for? We don't want to ruin Christmas.' My parents would have all sorts of systems in place, everything but the laser trip-wire, but I'd ransack the house and find it all. At the same time, I'd hate my brother and sister's birthdays, because I was a Christmas baby and it never seemed like I had a birthday. My parents ended up buying me a present as well, just so I didn't kick off.

We all played together and were close, but apart from the fact that I looked like my brother, it was like I was a different breed. Justin, the middle sibling, was the one we took the piss out of for being a swot. When I was getting some mad game for Christmas, he was getting a computer. Personality-wise, I was closer to my sister Ashley, although we were always quite different. But it was after I was attacked by the chimpanzee that I really started going off the rails and those differences became more obvious.

The day that turned out to be such a pivotal moment in my life had started so innocuously. It was a boiling hot morning in the summer holidays and my brother and I were stuck for something to do. James Stafford, my brother's best mate who lived a few streets away, knocked us up and asked if we wanted to go swimming. Mum got our kit ready and soon we were making our way to the baths.

Crossing the Ferry Bridge over the River Trent, we noticed some big tops being set up on some waste ground. The circus had come to town. Swimming was suddenly out of the window, because when you're a ten-year-old kid, the circus coming to town is just about the best thing ever. My heart started racing and our pace quickened.

We asked the guy on the entrance if we could see the animals, to which he replied, 'Yeah, of course, all the animals are on chains. You boys will be fine.' Inside the first big top we came to was an elephant. Inside the second were some little monkeys, who showed me their fangs when I got too close. I was in my own little world, and at some point became separated from my brother and James.

Then I came across the baby chimpanzee in the clearing. What happened next would impact the rest of my life in unthinkable ways. That attack lasted such a short amount of time but was like a tiny stone being thrown into a big pond, causing ripples that last to this day.

Having seen off the chimp, I experienced a moment of elation, followed by a burst of relief. But the relief was short-lived. When I looked down, I could see blood spattered all over me. Then the whole place erupted.

I was discovered by one of the circus workers, and I can still picture her face as she placed her hand on the back of my arm. It was a look of horror, partly because of the severity of my wounds and partly, I suspect, because she knew there could be a legal case against the circus. Part of my right forearm had been torn away. There was stringy white muscle and what I assume were tendons hanging off it. It looked like a bone that had been slobbered over by a dog all day. My other arm was covered in bites. I was not a pretty sight.

Before I knew it, I was in an ambulance being rushed to a local hospital. Meanwhile, James, who was a bit of a chubby lad, was running back to my house to tell my mum the news. He'd never run so fast and probably hasn't done since. When my mum answered the door, James was standing there red-faced and out of breath. My poor mum had been enjoying a rare day off work, kid-free, and suddenly there was someone standing on her doorstep informing her that her son had been attacked by a chimpanzee. How on earth do you react to that? I think it's safe to say that she was somewhat taken aback.

I was turned away from the hospital, presumably because they didn't have the correct facilities – to be fair, chimp attacks were quite rare in Burton-on-Trent in 1980 – and at the second hospital they made a complete hash of the treatment. They should have done a skin graft. Instead, they put stitches all around the wound and yanked it tight. It was never going to heal like that. When they removed the bandage a couple of weeks later, the doctor cut the first stitch and the wound burst open, like a badly packed kebab. But all they did was re-stitch and re-dress it and send me on my way.

About a week later, we went to France for a family holiday. That was the worst holiday ever. Every day, I'd have to watch my brother and sister playing in the sea, while I sat on the beach with a plastic bag over my arm. We were staying in a caravan and one day my father was maniacally cleaning up. As he was going about his business, he picked up an unusual smell. He couldn't work out what it was, it was driving him mad. He was traipsing up and down the caravan getting stressed, putting bleach down the toilet and the sink. I was lying out on the sofa, reading a book, when he homed in on my arm like a bloodhound and started sniffing me. Suddenly, he took my arm, removed the bag and unwound the bandage. And there, on my arm, were all these green spots. Gangrene had set in, followed by panic.

My dad called a taxi, bundled me in the back and we set off for Saint-Tropez. About an hour later, we arrived at the surgery and they got me straight into a room and onto a bed. The doctor told my dad to get on top of me and hold me down, and suddenly my dad was on the bed with his knee in my chest. It was like a scene from an 18th-century battle, back when surgeons would climb on top of casualties and chop limbs off without anaesthetic.

The doctor grabbed what looked like a scrubbing brush, covered it in ethanol and started scouring my arm, as if it was a frying pan caked in burnt-on food. I can still hear my screaming now. They must have been able to hear it as far away as Paris. It was pure torture, almost as traumatic as being attacked by the chimp. And it felt like my dad was one of my torturers.

After I'd been patched up and dosed up with antibiotics, the doctor led us to a different part of the surgery, a beautiful room with high, painted ceilings. Probably because he felt a bit guilty about what he'd just done to his son, the doctor introduced my dad to a glamorous lady with a blond beehive and they kissed each other cheek to cheek. No doubt, my dad also threw in the odd line of Del Boy French. This woman was stunning, but I wasn't interested. I was a ten-year-old boy who had just been scrubbed free of gangrene, which was the worst pain I'd ever experienced. All I wanted at that moment was a hug, some much-needed love from my father. But it never came. Not then, not later.

My dad paid the bill, which was probably a horrific amount of money, we said our goodbyes, and I noticed that while my dad didn't seem at all interested about what I'd just been through, he seemed absolutely elated about something. When we were out on the street, he looked down at me with wide, star-struck eyes and said, 'Son, I can't believe it. I just met Bridget Bardot.'

I had no idea who this woman was. It was like some weird black comedy: one scene I was being attacked by a chimpanzee, the next I was having my gangrenous arm scrubbed, the next I was meeting a famous French film star. Or at least my dad was. When Dad told my mum the story, he was overcome with excitement. It seemed to me as if the chimp attack and hospital trauma had all been worth it, because he had got to meet Bridget Bardot.

* * *

After leaving prep school, I was sent to Abbot Beyne, which was a comprehensive in Burton. I looked back at my time at St Wystan's, which was a feeder school for the prestigious Repton, and realised just how privileged I'd been. Even now, I have a passion for that kind of private schooling, the kind that pushes its pupils. My brother, sister and I were quite posh, and that made us stick out like sore thumbs in state school. I wasn't really in with the cool kids, although I was comfortable with that. I had a few friends at school and the little clique I was part of was high enough up the food chain that I never got bullied. We were all kind of well-to-do, from middle-class families with nice houses. It turned me into a bit of a closet snob and reinforced the idea that I was different. Not only that, I liked the fact that I was different.

I was the only pupil to wear a double-breasted blazer when most of the other kids were happy to wear a blazer with the arms and pockets hanging off. I got my love of clothes from my dad, who always looked impeccable. Actually, I didn't share this trait just with Dad, because my step-brother Mark, from my dad's first marriage, was also a smart dresser. Mark always looked cool, had a pretty girlfriend and even drove a Capri Ghia. I looked up to him and we always stayed close.

Me and my mates were all into the Mod and Ska scene – the Jam, Madness, the Beat. I had this beautiful pair of black-and-white shoes that I had to hide from my dad, because he had a very clear idea of how I should and shouldn't dress. I'd sneak clothes out of the house in a plastic bag and get changed around the corner. But when I look back at old photos now, I realise I didn't really look much like Paul Weller or Suggs. To be honest, I just looked a bit pathetic.

I was good at some things as a kid, including art. One day, my brother bought the 12-inch version of 'Relax' by Frankie Goes to

Hollywood, the one featuring a muscly bloke with a woman on his back, with pointy tits and wearing thigh-high boots. I drew it and thought it was brilliant. A few days later, I came home from school and couldn't find my drawing. My dad had found it and torn it up, because it was sexual and he found it disgusting.

Other times, he'd give me a good hiding. It was just slaps with the back of his hand and I don't resent him for that. You could argue some kids nowadays could do with something similar. But at the time, so much resentment had built up that I'd come to despise him. After another incident, the details of which slip my mind, I came out of my bedroom in tears and said, 'I fucking hate that cunt.' Unbeknown to me, he was standing on the landing. I backed into a corner, thinking I was going to get a beating, but instead he gave me a cuddle.

It was a bizarre moment, the only time I remember anything like that happening and harbouring any affection for him. Unfortunately, it felt like he was uncomfortable doing it, so it was hard to receive. When someone who's normally cold suddenly starts hugging you or saying nice things, your natural reaction is to think that something's not quite right.

Then, when I was 13, my dad upped and left, just disappeared one day without any explanation. I'm told he phoned Mum from the airport, told her he was leaving and wouldn't be coming back again. It was extremely traumatic for my mum, especially because her parents, who I had also been very close to, had recently died within three months of each other. She was lumbered with three kids, a big house and a crippling mortgage, because my dad refused to give her any money. Mum tells me now that she was having to steal toilet roll from work to make ends meet. I wrote my dad letters, telling him we couldn't afford to go out or buy clothes, but he wasn't interested.

My mum never bad-mouthed him in front of us, but I later learned that he'd always been a bit of a player. You can try to read too much into relationship breakdowns. Sometimes it's as simple as your dad meeting someone else and deciding that being with her would be more fun. The grass is always greener. When times got tough, he decided that the best solution was to walk out, close the door and disappear. I didn't understand it at the time, but I'd end up doing something similar.

I didn't share my mum's distress at my dad's departure. As far as I was concerned, it was the best thing that had ever happened to me. It was like a massive weight had fallen from my shoulders. That's not how most kids react when their father walks out. But just because I thought Dad leaving was great, that didn't mean it was good for everyone around me. Suddenly the shackles were off, and I could live as I wanted to. That meant complete and utter mayhem.

3

LOSING BATTLE

Everything in the Royal Marines was done to extremes. People were forever trying to prove themselves, taking things as close to what was acceptable as possible, which often meant going miles over it. It wasn't uncommon to see a load of Marines knocking ten bells of shit out of civvies down the local pub. But that wasn't enough, they'd have to be doing it dressed as old women. I didn't get enjoyment out of fighting, that was never really my thing, but I still had immense pride in being part of the brotherhood.

We always said that the Royal Marines is the hardest gang in the world. When you were together with the lads, in whatever situation, you knew that there would always be someone to your left, someone to your right, someone above and below you. I loved being part of one of the military's inner circles, but I also liked being a stray, floating in and out of the group without anyone taking offence or questioning my loyalty.

When I joined 45 Commando, we had what was called 'rig', which was what we were 'supposed' to wear on a night out. It consisted of jeans, a T-shirt and desert boots. It was effectively a uniform, but I'd never wear it. As far as I was concerned, I did my job, but it was up to me what I did after that. The commanding officers weren't bothered what I wore, but there was some friction from some of the old sweats, the guys who had been there longer and thought a fellow Marine having his own identity was a bit suspicious.

I was 19 when I went on my first tour to Northern Ireland in 1990. After weeks of beat-up training, we were sent to Bessbrook Mill in County Armagh, which was where some of the worst violence of the Troubles took place and was bona fide bandit country. Every British soldier in Northern Ireland had a price on their head, and that price was a lot higher for a green (Royal Marine) or red (Parachute Regiment) beret. Not that I cared about any of that. I'd joined the military to see action. I was wide-eyed with excitement at the possibility of coming into contact with the IRA. To be honest, anything less would have been a disappointment.

I'd been through the training and flicked through the brochures lying around the mess hall, with their photos of smiling soldiers hoisting the British flag in newly secured compounds or posing with their weapons, but none of that prepares you for war. The IRA knew we were coming and wanted to welcome us with a bang. But when our squadron landed to take over from the Coldstream Guards, the place was already a mess. Someone from the IRA had driven into a vehicle checkpoint and detonated a 500-pound bomb. They thought the changeover had already taken place and the Royal Marines were manning the checkpoint. Fortunately for us boys, they'd got their intelligence wrong.

The compound had been blown to bits and the sky was thick with smoke. As we were picking through the wreckage, the sergeant in charge kicked a blackened helmet and said, 'Right, lads, the first thing we need to do is see if we can find any more of these.' At first, I didn't know what he meant. But when I looked down at the helmet he'd kicked, I realised it still had a head strapped inside it. The sergeant had been in the Falklands and presumably seen a lot of bad things, which might explain his nonchalance. But for me, that was a big wake-up call. Military life had little to do with hoisting flags and posing for photos with smiles on your faces. This was war and it was time for me to grow up.

When people were at home watching the Troubles on TV, they only saw one side, which was the British Army on the streets. It's not as if we were going at it with the IRA on a battlefield. That's why people outside of the military often refer to the Troubles as an uprising or terrorist campaign. But to me and the rest of the British military, it was a war. And it was definitely a war to the IRA.

But while seeing things like a decapitated head in a helmet was a massive shock, people were always ready to make a joke out of any situation. You'd shut your experience in a box, lock it away, get shitfaced, forget about it and move on. It was almost as if it hadn't happened. That's not a good way of dealing with things long term. But what you've also got to bear in mind is that I wanted to see action every day. I was gagging for it. I wanted it to kick off, for us to be attacked and for us to attack them. That's what I signed up for. I'd gone from boy to man in a heartbeat, it was an incredibly steep growth, but it was also incredibly exciting. This was the thrill I'd been chasing all my life.

We were attacked 19 times in six months, but not one of us got killed. One guy stepped on a pressure plate near an IED and was blown across a field. But while his weapon was bent, he was only slightly injured. One night, there was another attack as a Chinook helicopter was bringing in new troops for a changeover. The IRA had got their timings wrong again, which meant there were two sets of troops on the ground at the same time. It all went off and the lads ended up putting fire down into the local town. Unfortunately, I wasn't there. I was listening to it from the operations room.

You might think it strange wanting to be there, but everyone felt like that, not just me. There is a strain of people in the world that thrives on that level of danger. People don't join the Royal Marines to sit around in camp all day, they join for conflict. Maggie Thatcher came out with a great quote about the Marines after the Falklands, something along the lines of: 'They need to be locked away in a container and brought out only in times of war.' That's just so true. Open up the container and we'd all come pouring out like gimps, waving our weapons and shouting, 'Where's the fucking battle?' So, when we heard the contacts coming over the radio, thousands and thousands of rounds going down on the enemy, we were all sitting around thinking, 'This is fucking brilliant – I wish I was there!' And when I saw the lads coming back, I was just so jealous.

The police put in checkpoints all around the area, so that anyone trying to get out would have to pass through them. Bizarrely, they were stopping people who had been shot in their cars – IRA members who had obviously been involved in the contact – and letting them go. Either they had to get medical assistance or didn't have any weapons on them. But I just couldn't understand it. We had a hit list, we knew the terrorists' faces, we were stopping them on a daily basis. I couldn't get my head around the fact that we knew who the enemy was but often weren't allowed to do anything about it.

Some lads became so frustrated they started pulling people out of cars and filling them in, but they got into big trouble for it. There were rules of engagement and rules of arrest, and one of the lads got sent away for a long time after getting carried away. If we didn't have solid grounds to apprehend them, we had to bite our lips and let them go. Even if we did have something specific to pin on them, we'd still let them go, because the powers that be were waiting to build a bigger case that might bring more people down with them.

Sometimes it's better to know who your enemy are and what they're up to than to take them off the ground. But I joined the Royal Marines to fight an enemy. I was only 19, I'd never thought about why I was there. I was just proud to be representing the UK, in troubled lands that we were trying to control. And then I had an epiphany. We'd slept rough for the night, I was marching down the street and there was a guy in my patrol with the ECM (electronic countermeasure) equipment on his back, which is used to jam explosive signals. But when I looked at him more closely, I could see that his weapon was all over the place and his earpiece was swinging down by his knees. I thought, 'What the fuck are you doing? That piece of equipment might save our lives.' Then I thought, 'All these missions they're giving us – to check this and that out, find IEDs under bridges – we're just being used as bait.'

I didn't have proof, I just had this overwhelming feeling that we were being put on the ground so that we might get attacked and the intelligence services could then come and build a picture. Because if there was no activity from the military, there wouldn't be any activity from the IRA. It was about knowing who the terrorists were but allowing them to do their thing. Because allowing them to do their thing – in other words, attack us – allowed the intelligence services to burrow down even further and possibly bust the whole operation. That's still my belief today, that infantry were expendable.

I understood the thinking, but it shattered the dreams I'd been having for five years. I started wondering what I'd signed up for and why I was there. I was losing my motivation, because I wanted to be at the sharp end every day. There wasn't enough going on, everything felt pointless. This was not what I'd day-dreamed about in maths class. I'd been inspired by what the lads had done in the Falklands, and this didn't match up to it.

I kept my suspicions to myself, because I knew they would be met with scorn. As far as I knew, no one else thought we were there as bait. This is one of the problems of being a non-conformist in the military, you think too much. After I left the military, I'd bump into old colleagues who'd say to me, 'I always remember you asking why.' That open questioning would come later, when I was more experienced and more secure. But even at the age of 19, everything had to have a reason for being.

I had this sudden realisation that if I wanted to be stimulated, do real soldiering and have a real impact, I'd have to join the Special Forces. Not that joining the Special Forces was a realistic option. At 19, I didn't think I was capable. I was leaning more towards leaving the military altogether. I was just so disillusioned with it all and I'd had enough of hoping it would get better.

After returning from that first tour, I went straight on leave. That was the part I enjoyed the most, letting my hair down and raising hell. I was in the pub with my old school mate and now fellow marine Mark Sherriff when Operation Desert Storm came on the news. Not long after that, my phone rang and I was on the train back to 45 Commando. Being recalled from leave was exactly what I needed. This was the real deal, exactly what I'd signed up for.

In Iraq, our task was to bring the Kurds down from the mountains, where they'd been driven by Saddam Hussein's forces. Before we went in, we were given medical training – how to put drips in, that sort of thing. That was the first time that had happened before an operation I'd been involved in, and it meant they were preparing us for casualties. There was a sense that this was a proper war and that we were going to face the enemy on the battlefield. It was a thrilling but scary thought.

I remember looking around and thinking, 'Some of these boys won't be coming back, and one of those boys might be me.' As it turned out, there was no aggressive action and no major conflict. All was well. And that was highly disappointing, because conflict was exactly what we'd wanted.

Not that we didn't see some horrible things in Iraq. In some of the villages, we found dead bodies with the limbs cut off and swapped over, so that the legs were coming out of the arm sockets and vice versa. It was a bizarre ritual and a barbarity and disrespect for fellow humans that was on a whole different level to anything we'd seen in Northern Ireland. As a recruit, you might prepare yourself for seeing dead soldiers, but you don't really prepare yourself for seeing civilians mutilated in that way. It was a mindfuck, but there had been absolutely no psychological preparation. There just weren't any mechanisms in place back then, pre- or post-war. You saw what you saw, did what you had to do, went on leave at the end of it and got drunk for a few weeks.

Showing any kind of negative emotion in the field simply wasn't allowed. In a warzone, that can be a weakness and can leave you vulnerable. As a soldier, you have to be resilient, you have to be able to bounce back from whatever you see or do and be on point immediately. That's an innate trait, dating back to when we lived in warring tribes, and when wallowing in grief simply wasn't an option when you were under attack and trying to survive. So we laughed about what we saw instead.

Iraq turned out to be disappointingly uneventful. We went in at the back end of the war, when most of the heavy lifting had already been done. And when I returned home, things really started to unravel. While on leave, I met my future wife, Helen. For a while, our relationship was great. I was physically attracted to her, she was fun and we shared a love of partying, so whenever we could we'd dance and drink until the early hours. It was just natural that I'd end up in a relationship with someone from that world. But when the music stopped and I had to return to work, cracks started to appear. To be in the military for any length of time, you need a very selfless partner, and it takes a very special woman to support your vocation, rather than tolerate or incessantly moan about it. Supporting and tolerating are two very different things.

I hadn't been in the Marines long before I started to seriously reconsider my future in the military. However, I decided to give things one last shot. So I thought I'd train myself up and prepare myself for Special Forces Selection in Poole. But I ended up doing menial soldiering duties on camp instead. It was mind-numbingly boring, I quickly lost interest and wound up putting in my notice to leave. This was only 1992, but it wasn't meeting my needs and I'd had enough. Peacetime soldiering was too small and mundane, I couldn't be doing with the petty bullshit: looking after my uniform, general duties, admin. That's why I spent so much time drinking and partying, because I found it more exciting.

I'd done about a year of my 18-month notice period when my brother Justin, who had decided to become a helicopter pilot, had his pass-out parade in Dartmouth. It was there that I met my old Marines officer Baggsy Baker, who sounds like he's stepped out of a Biggles story but was someone I greatly respected. We had a good chat about my time in Iraq and when he asked what my plans were, I told him I was leaving. He was taken aback. When I explained that I'd never found my feet in the military and nothing was meeting my needs, he replied, 'Mate, do not leave. You've got what it takes to join the Special Forces. If you leave now, you'll regret it for the rest of your life.'

His words started me thinking. As a kid, I'd been transfixed by TV images of the Iranian Embassy siege in London, when mysterious men in black balaclavas had abseiled down the building, smashed through windows and destroyed the terrorists. Those images were the greatest recruitment tool the Special Forces possessed. But they also had the opposite effect, in that they made joining the Special Forces feel like a pipe dream. In my mind, the Special Forces was a world inhabited by soldier-gods, James Bond types who jumped off cliffs and wrestled sharks just to deliver a box of Milk Tray. Consequently, I didn't think I had it in me to pass the training. But someone I respected showing that kind of faith in me bolstered my confidence, made me feel that the impossible might be possible. It's amazing how a chance meeting and a few short words can be so inspiring. Baggsy got in touch recently, and I told him that he set me on the path. If it hadn't been for that conversation, I would never have done what I've done.

When I got back to Poole, I had a long, hard think and decided to go for it. The first thing I had to do was take out my notice to leave. To do so, I had to see the sergeant I was working for at the time, who was this big, fat knacker. I fucking hated him, and as far as he was concerned, I was the worst soldier he had, because I didn't do as I was told.

When I walked into his office and told him I wanted to withdraw my notice and put in for Special Boat Service (SBS) Selection, he looked at me and burst out laughing.

'I cannot believe this,' he said. 'This is fucking brilliant! It's made my day! I'm definitely going to put you forward, because I can't wait to see you back here in a few weeks' time. This is going to be hilarious...'

What this officer didn't know was that if you doubt me, I'll do everything in my power to prove you wrong and make you look stupid.

4

SHOTGUN WILLY

t's too easy to pinpoint one specific event and say, 'That's why I am who I am.' It wasn't just being attacked by a chimpanzee that turned me loopy. I'd always been a loose cannon, always felt the need to put myself into dangerous situations in order to feel alive. But there is no doubt that the chimp attack, combined with my father upping and leaving, amplified things, right up to 11.

I went at life hell for leather, constantly searching for extreme experiences and chasing threats, because the alternative seemed mediocre and boring. I think that came from coming so close to losing my life. I was an angry little kid, would snap in a heartbeat. I knew that wasn't normal, I knew that made me different from most other kids. I wasn't outwardly that way, not so that people would be wary around me. But there was this turbulent anger swirling around inside me, like a silent storm. My brother and sister were the opposite, especially Justin, who seemed to have achieved amazing things quite effortlessly. The only reason I can think of for why I'm the way I am and they're the way they are is that neither Justin nor Ashley were attacked by an angry chimp.

There wasn't an immediate reaction to the attack, but it didn't take me long to start getting up to no good. I was always the one who would push things to the limit, whose mates would be saying, 'Really? Are you sure you want to do that?' Some of the stuff I got up to was just ridiculous. I bought a crossbow and would fire bolts into the sky, in the direction of my brother and his mates at the other end of the field. I thought it was hilarious, watching them scattering and running away, not sparing a thought about what might happen if a bolt landed on one of their heads. There was also an incident where I burnt down a barn. The barn was next to our house and full of hay. I found some matches, started messing about with them and skulked off. The next thing I knew, the barn was up in flames and billowing smoke. In no time at all, it had been razed to the ground and there were fire engines everywhere. My dad knew I had been up there, but I never put my hand up and said it was me.

I had no value for life or concept of how my actions might have terrible consequences for somebody else. I had no empathy, was almost emotionless in terms of the effect my behaviour was having on the people around me.

One day at school, one of my mates said, 'Lads, I've got the keys to the doctor's house across the road from where I live...' It transpired he'd done some baby-sitting and never given the keys back. It was this beautiful country house and he'd already been in a few times to nick food, rifle through drawers and generally mooch around. When he asked me to join him on a raid, it felt like I was being invited into the inner circle.

We rode up to the house on our bikes, let ourselves in, ransacked the fridge, stole a bit of change out of the fruit basket and ran riot all over the rooms. I was only 14, it was naughty and we shouldn't have been doing it, but it was nothing too sinister or malicious. Around the same time, I'd started shoplifting, not for the financial reward, just for the buzz. This was the same. The buzz didn't come from stealing food or the odd quid here and there, it came from the possibility of being caught, because we knew the doctor and his family could return home at any time.

The following afternoon, we pushed a little bit further. It was a massive house and easy to get lost in, and I found myself alone in the master bedroom. Sensing there might be something interesting under the bed, I got down on my hands and knees, lifted the valance and stuck my head underneath. And there it was: an antique shotgun, one of the loveliest things I'd ever laid eyes on.

I'd always loved weapons, whether it was axes or penknives or catapults. And the less interested I became in schoolwork, the more I just wanted to be out in nature, handling tools and running wild. When other kids were reading the *Beano*, I was reading *Combat and Survival*. I loved playing in the woods and was in the Scouts and Adventure Club, before I got kicked out for making a clay cock and showing it to all the girls.

So when I clapped eyes on this beautiful gun, my head started spinning. It was like that scene from *Pulp Fiction*, when John Travolta opens the briefcase, his mouth falls open and it looks like he might faint. I shoved the shotgun back under the bed and thought, 'My God, what have I found?' I was smitten, but I was also scared, because I knew that handling guns usually didn't end well.

I didn't even mention it to the other boys, but I told my brother about it when I went home that night and he was almost as excited as me. That was all the encouragement I needed, and I told him I was going to nick it the following evening. And that's exactly what I did. I had this fishtail parka, with arms down to my knees, but it was the perfect coat for concealing a shotgun. I made my escape on this little racing bike, and as I freewheeled downhill, the shotgun that was almost as long as me pressed against my body, I felt like a million dollars. I had no idea what I was going to do with the shotgun. I just had to have it.

As soon as I got home, I went to the stable, stuck the shotgun in a vice and sawed the stock off with a hacksaw. It was madness. This thing was absolutely beautiful and it must have cost a fortune, and here I was sawing it in half as if I was a bank robber about to do a job. A lot of people ask, 'How the hell did you know how to saw a shotgun down?' Because my dad had been working me so hard, getting me to cut wood, copper pipes and everything else, cutting down a shotgun was second nature to me. I even finished it perfectly, so that there were no sharp edges. They would have ruined my coat. I didn't do any bank jobs, and for a while I just carried the shotgun about with me, under my parka. Even took it to school one day and hid it in my locker. Just doing that gave me a massive buzz.

I'd recently seen *Rambo*, and that's who I wanted to be like. So I got my brother to buy a load of shotgun shells from the local hardware store, as well as a gun belt and a 15-inch knife. I hid the shotgun in my mum's walk-in wardrobe and at night we'd go out on little missions. We'd go to a car park, sneak up on people necking in the back seat, chuck stones at the windows, wait for the guy to come out, point the shotgun at him and fire it over his head. There were flames coming out of the barrel and these big men would start shrieking, jump straight back into their cars and drive off at 100mph.

I thought it was brilliant, just harmless fun. I had no concept that what I was doing might get me into trouble or have psychological consequences for the poor people I was firing over. I had never handled a firearm and had no idea what I was doing. I could have quite easily killed the person I was firing it over, myself or the person standing next to me. I just didn't care, it didn't even enter my head. All I cared about was pushing and pushing to the absolute limit.

One day, I said to my mum, 'A friend of mine's got some duck, do you want some bringing back?'

'Oh yes, Matt, that would be lovely.'

I went down to a pond near the house, started blazing away at these ducks and pumped one full of pellets. When I returned home that night, I tossed this duck on the kitchen table in triumph, as if I was some hardened hunter. She was expecting it to be plucked, gutted and dressed. She knew something fishy was going on, she just wasn't sure what.

I always had a lot of friends who were older than me, including one boy called Johnny who lived down the street. We used to go to a barber shop owned by a guy we knew and sit drinking tea and chatting, a bit like that sitcom *Desmond's*. But when I decided I needed money to buy some bullets, we broke in one night and nicked the cash box, which contained about 200 quid. And when you're 14, 200 quid is an absolute fortune.

After we got the big haul from the hairdresser's, I told my friends I was going to take them for a celebratory day out. I filled a duffle bag with all my Rambo gear, ordered a taxi and we went off to the country for a shooting trip. But as soon as we got out there, I fired one round off and every bird within miles flew out of the trees and scarpered. Suddenly, we had nothing to do.

While the other boys traipsed off home, I went to the playing fields and had a lie down in some long grass next to the river, cradling the shotgun as if it was a lover. It was a beautiful day. The sun was beating down, there was a nice breeze and the grass was blowing all around me. Then, all of a sudden, I heard someone coming. I looked up to see a girl standing over me and smirking. I knew that smug face. Every school has a 'worst' family, and in my school it was the Mitchells. While my family were considered to be snobs, because we lived in a big house and spoke funny, they were at the other end of the spectrum. Like us, the Mitchells consisted of two brothers and a sister, but they were weird as hell. There were stories about them sacrificing cats in a graveyard. But worse, as far as I was concerned, was that they used to pick on my sister. And it just so happened that the girl standing over me was the Mitchell sister.

She started taking the piss out of me, calling me a cowboy and asking me who the hell I thought I was. I wasn't having any of that. I loaded the shotgun, swung it in her direction and squeezed off two rounds directly above her head. You won't be surprised to learn that she shat herself. As she ran through the flood plain, her high heels flew off and she looked like Moses, parting the Red Sea. Apart from James Stafford after the chimpanzee attack, I'd never seen anyone move so fast.

After another couple of hours sunbathing with my beloved shotgun, I finally went home. I sneaked past my mum, who was pottering in the garden, slipped into the house and hid the shotgun in her wardrobe. A couple of hours later, I was messing about in the stables – probably up to no good – when I heard voices and my mum shouting my name. When I peered through this big gate with square openings at the top, I saw her talking to a couple of policemen. Poor Mum had been doing a nice spot of gardening on a Sunday afternoon, and now she was dealing with the long arm of the law.

When I finally showed myself, one of the policemen said to me, 'Matt, we believe you're in possession of a sawn-off shotgun.'

'Nah, you've got it wrong, I haven't got a shotgun.'

'Matt, if you don't tell us where it is, we're going to have to arrest you.'

'Arrest me? Really?'

At that point, I thought I should probably tell them where the shotgun was. I took them into the house, went up the stairs and into my mum's bedroom. She, of course, was baffled. I brought the shotgun out, handed it to the police and thought that would be the end of it: 'Oh, thanks Matt, cheers for being so cooperative, see you later.' Instead, my mum fainted on the spot and I was put into the back of a police car and taken down to the station.

I didn't understand what I'd done that was so serious. I just thought I'd been having a bit of fun. Hours and hours of interviews ensued, but I didn't tell them everything, because that would have meant snitching on the other lads. I made up a story about finding the shotgun on some waste ground, where my dogs had sniffed it out. They believed me, why wouldn't they? How else was a kid going to get his hands on a sawn-off shotgun? Plus, I'd done a great job at cutting it down. How would a kid know how to do that? It's not as if I was known to associate with villains from London's East End.

The police mistakenly connected the shotgun to a load of post office robberies that had taken place in the local area and everything was done and dusted. I'd bluffed the police, not got my mates in the shit and got away with it. The whole episode had been a buzz, a lot of fun. But the police aren't that stupid.

A few weeks later, the mum of the kid who had got us into the house found a cheque from the doctor in his bedroom. She confronted him, told the doctor and it all started to unravel. The doctor told the police, an inventory was done, and they discovered the shotgun was missing from under the doctor's bed. I'd been rumbled. Me and the other lads, including my brother, were taken in for questioning and the police soon pieced the picture together. It looked nothing like what I'd told them, so I had to admit what I'd done.

After a weekend in the cells I was let out on the Monday. By that time, the penny had finally dropped: I was deep in the shit. But while I waited for the wheels of justice to turn, I went about my normal business. I had a paper round and an *Advertiser* round on the biggest hill in town. I'd deliver both up the hill, switching between both sides of the road, before freewheeling all the way down. My bike had dodgy brakes, so normally when I got about 100 metres from the bottom, I'd start slowing down, so that by the time I reached the traffic lights, the bike would stop. The morning after being released by the police, I was bombing down this hill, thinking about all the horrible things I could do to the Mitchell girl as revenge for grassing on me and picking on my sister. And just as I started braking, someone stepped out from in front of a car and I slammed into them. This person was draped over my handlebars, staring straight at me, and I quickly realised it was the Mitchell girl. Both of us were screaming, I was looking at her thinking, 'Oh my God, it's you!', and she was looking at me thinking the same thing.

We must have travelled about 100 metres together, before we came to a halt and ended up in a heap all over the road. An ambulance came, whisked her off to hospital (she was okay, just a few cuts and bruises) and I was taken back in for questioning. The police thought it had been an assassination attempt, to silence her. What a way to try to get rid of someone! I said to the police, 'Do you think I'm that stupid – or that accurate – to be sitting at the top of the hill, taking note of the distance and wind speed, muttering to myself, "As long as I maintain 31 miles per hour, I should hit the target bang on the money..."?'

I managed to persuade them, but even after all that, I still had to push things. A week later, I stole a motorbike before shoplifting a pair of jeans by putting them on under my trousers. The owner caught me, called the police, and the copper was the same one who had arrested me for nicking the shotgun. He walked through the door of the shop, saw me and said, 'Oh, for fuck's sake, not you again. I can't believe you're still doing this shit!' It had got to the stage where my mum was on first-name terms with the policemen. One of them, Neil, would phone her at work and say, 'Angela, we've got him again', and she'd have to trudge down to the police station. She'd say to me, 'For goodness' sake, Matt, just stop it!' But I didn't know how.

At the police station, having been apprehended for attempting to nick the jeans, they were all calling me 'Shotgun Willy'. The copper who arrested me took me down to the cells and said, 'Look, I'm sure your father will pay bail. But the alternative is a remand home.'

Straightaway I replied, 'I'd rather go to a remand home.'

I couldn't face my father, I knew it would be a hideous scene. So off I went by choice to the remand home.

Not long before, my dad had made me watch the 1970s' film *Scum* about the brutality of life in a British borstal, and said, 'That's where you'll end up if you're not careful.' But I thought *Scum* was exaggerated. I wasn't scared of remand home. I thought I'd be top dog, have the most charisma and the best clothes and that people would be bowing down to me.

It turned out that *Scum* was actually quite realistic. My remand home wasn't quite a prison, but it felt like one to a 14-year-old kid. People from my background weren't supposed to get into this kind of trouble and kids like me weren't supposed to end up in a remand home. I was scared shitless.

5

SO NEAR, SO FAR

You have to have an operational tour under you belt and a couple of years' experience in the military to be able to put yourself forward for Special Forces Selection. But the bosses can still say no if they don't think you're up to it. However, my boss wasn't going to stand in my way, because he wanted to see me fail so much. God, that would have provided him with so much joy.

I had four weeks to go until SBS Selection in Poole, and I spent that time map-reading and training with packs on my back, so that I had whipped myself into pretty good shape by the time it came to joining up. The instructions were to meet at 06:00 hours at the boat store, with a length of rope and a tyre, which we had to source ourselves. When I rocked up, I was eyeing all these super-soldiers who looked the business – some of them huge, some of them ripped, some of them with cold, dead eyes – and I thought, 'Fucking hell, did I get off the wrong bus? Maybe I won't make it...'

It soon became apparent that we would be towing the tyre behind us wherever we went, through water, sand, mud and bushes. There were fitness tests and load marches, swimming assessments, map and compass skills. It was all about telling us exactly what would be expected of us, should we make it into Special Forces.

For two weeks, we got thrashed beyond belief, while getting hardly any sleep and never knowing what was going to happen next. There were marches across hills and a lot of boat work with collapsible canoes, often covering huge distances through tidal waters. It wasn't uncommon for us to be woken up for a 'beasting', which meant being dragged from a state of sleep into a savage physical and psychological thrashing in a matter of seconds. One day, we were herded into an auditorium and told to grab a shower. When we filed back into the auditorium, the heating was cranked up to full blast and we were made to watch a forklift truck moving different coloured barrels from one stack to another. We were supposed to keep tabs on the order the barrels were placed in, to replicate being in an observation post in a hot Middle Eastern country. When you've been travelling for days, you're tired and hungry, the sun is roaring and all you want to do is sleep, you still have to be switched on, because what appear to be mundane goings on can actually be vital intelligence for friendly forces. But as the minutes ticked by, all I could hear in the auditorium was heads smashing against desks as fatigue did its thing.

Any soldier that puts himself forward for Selection obviously thinks he's fit enough, and they could smash the physical stuff all day long, if it wasn't for the mental torture: taking away their sleep, making them hungry, messing with their norms.

Passing Selection is not about being the fittest or the strongest, it's about who keeps going, no matter what you come up against. It's not about being miles ahead on a march, it's about plodding along in the pack and still being there at the end. The natural inclination for an alpha male – and you get a lot of alpha males in the military – is to want to shout about what you are made of. But wanting to be at the front of the pack is more about your ego than anything else. Why would you want to stand out? As soon as you start showing off, trying to let people know that you're the fittest or the strongest, all eyes are on you. And those eyes will start looking for a whole range of potential weaknesses. Although, of course, you don't want to be at the back either.

In the Special Forces, this ability to appear unremarkable so as not to draw attention to yourself is called being 'the grey man'. The public perception of a Special Forces soldier and the reality are very different. You might walk into a bar full of soldiers, see a load of musclebound lads swilling beer and being loud and assume that they are Special Forces. But the Special Forces lads are more likely to be short and wiry and sitting quietly in the corner.

Another day, we had to march with our collapsible canoes on our backs for what seemed like an eternity. That night, they took us into camp and said, 'Right, lads, get yourselves a shower and get your heads down.' I'd just nodded off when I was woken by a loud bang. The lights were on and an envelope was lying in the middle of the room. Someone opened it up and announced that we all had to be at a certain rendezvous point (RV) in 15 minutes. We were all gathered around this map, trying to work out where we needed to go, and eventually we came to the reluctant conclusion that the coordinates corresponded to the middle of a lake. So at about 3am, we all got our gear on, located the lake and swam into the middle of it.

We were treading water, waiting for the next instruction and freezing our tits off, when a head breached the surface, with a scuba mask on. Whoever it was handed us the next grid, before disappearing below the surface again. I was so sleep-deprived, I thought I might have been dreaming. I've got no doubt the training team sit around laughing about the weird stuff they come up with to test us. Then again, war is unpredictable and the situations you find yourself in can be very surreal.

Being in the Marines was all about the red mist and roaring into things at 100mph. But this was different. Another night, as we were marching, a car drove past. Shortly afterwards, we were stopped and asked what the car's registration was. Nobody had a clue. We then got thrashed beyond any thrashing I'd had before. And the whole time, the directing staff (DS) were shouting, 'You will pay attention to detail! This is fucking real, this is the thinking man's world, wake the fuck up!'

It was being drummed into us remorselessly that we needed to pay attention to every little detail at all times. Even details that might seem totally irrelevant might fit into the bigger picture. It was about having 360-degree awareness of everything we were doing. After that, I made a point of memorising the number plate of every car that went past me. I still do. That's how hard they hammer things into you during Selection.

In the Special Forces, we're constantly testing ourselves across a range of harsh environments and operating in the jungle is soldiering to a tee. The jungle is hot and humid, and whenever the heavens open, it becomes hellish. It's also very claustrophobic, because you're operating under a canopy of trees and among dense foliage. It's raw, the conditions are brutal, and it separates those who can function in incredibly difficult conditions from those who can't. *I'm a Celebrity... Get Me Out of Here!* it isn't.

During jungle acclimatisation training, we were thrashed every morning on the beach, and only then were we helicoptered in to do our work. The only luxury we had was a toothbrush and some toothpaste, the rest was soldiering kit. Generally speaking, you don't move in the jungle at night, that's when you try to get some sleep. And before getting your head down, you build your hammock in the pitch black of the jungle, take off all your wet kit, put it in a stuff sack, pack the stuff sack away, and get into your dry kit. Putting on that dry kit is one of the best feelings imaginable, like slipping into a bespoke suit in a Savile Row tailors. In stark contrast, when you wake before dawn the following morning, you have to drag yourself out of your hammock, take off that beautiful, crisp, dry kit and dig out all that horrible, stinking wet kit. When you open the stuff sack, the smell of body odour and ammonia punches you in the face. It might sound melodramatic, given everything else a Special Forces hopeful has to go through, but putting it on again is one of the worst things I've ever done. I'd imagine I was putting on a freshly ironed shirt and a pair of Armani jeans, while saying to myself, 'These are the nicest, most comfortable jeans you'll ever wear. When you get these on you'll feel a million dollars and look even better...' That's the only way I could get through it every morning, fooling myself it was a treat.

The jungle takes a soldier to his absolute limit. There was basic soldiering – two hands on your weapon at all times, camouflage cream on at all times – contact drills, survival and weapons skills and navigation, which is incredibly difficult. There are no roads or churches or schools, you're handed a green map with contour lines all over it and you have to work off ridge lines to know where you are. And all the while you're being hammered, day in, day out.

We also had to perform personal medical procedures, which were absolutely essential. Working in the jungle meant being exposed to insect bites and cuts, which had to be looked after constantly. And the dampness between your toes can lead to horrible sores. After a few weeks in the jungle, your feet can turn into two stumps of peeling mush and walking can become impossible. Many hopefuls have failed the jungle because they didn't look after the basics.

When I was in camp, admin drove me bonkers, but as soon as it served a purpose, I loved it. As well as a love of clothes, I inherited my obsession with order from my dad, who was always tidying up and making sure everything was in its right place, so it came quite naturally to me. In the jungle, if you're unable to take care of your weapon, your kit or yourself, you'll fail. Those small mistakes, such as disregarding the condition of your weapon or not replacing the button on your map pocket, can turn out to be catastrophic. Any cut can turn into an infection in a heartbeat, any equipment failure can soon turn into a mini-crisis, so you have to be right on top of everything. All your personal stuff has to be squared away, before you think about the tactical side of things.

The Special Forces operate like a crack rugby or football team, with the guys rather than the officers running the show. As such, the Special Forces need people with basic human skills, like resilience, intuition, being able to think on your feet and make snap decisions under intense pressure. If the hills chip away at a soldier's façade, operating in the jungle tears it down. Being in the jungle is like being an insect under a giant magnifying glass, and only the best don't get burnt. If you can survive the jungle, you know you've got what it takes to be a Special Forces operator.

Continuation training consisted of boating, blowing things up, learning Morse code, helicopter assault drills, forward abseiling down buildings and through windows and getting absolutely shitfaced. But not necessarily in that order. This was exactly what I'd joined up for and exactly how I'd imagined it would be. When you're handed that black kit, it must be the same feeling footballers or rugby players get when they're first handed an England strip.

A lot of SBS training was done side by side with the SAS, and there was a lot of friction between us at the time, similar to that between the Marines and the Paras. The SAS are a lot of guys who don't know each other suddenly thrown together, whereas it was a natural progression to go from the Marines into the SBS, so a lot of us already knew each other well. The SAS candidates were envious of that closeness.

Out in the wilds again, we were taught how to live off the land, by constructing shelters, starting fires, purifying water and improvising makeshift weapons. One fine day, a DS who had been blown up in Northern Ireland, and was one of the hardest, most horrible bastards I've ever met, dragged a sheep from the back of a trailer, shoved his hands in its mouth, pulled its head back and plunged a big knife into its neck. The sheep looked pretty upset, but the DS's face also contorted into a terrible expression, because the knife had gone through the sheep's neck and into his thigh. We all thought it was the best thing we'd ever seen, while the DS cracked on as if nothing had happened, despite claret spurting from his leg. He was like the Black Knight from *Monty Python and the Holy Grail*: ''Tis but a scratch...'

Almost before I'd had time to skin, cook and eat the sheep, I was in a barn with a hood over my head, stark naked, with my hands placed firmly on a table. I heard the snap of a rubber glove behind me, was told to brace and the next thing I knew I had been penetrated. Don't worry, it wasn't some weird Special Forces kink – like dressing up as women is to the Royal Marines – they were searching for contraband. Whatever their reasons, I don't recommend it – just as I don't envy the penetrator.

Having been thrown back out onto the hills, we slept by day and travelled by night, covering long distances navigating by the stars under the cover of darkness. Each time we reached a checkpoint, an agent would show up, parcel out stale bread and mouldy cheese and provide us with another set of coordinates. It sounds brutal, and it was. The constant pressure of being caught was horrible. We'd been given dog demos beforehand, during which we were wearing the protection sleeves. But we were told in no uncertain terms that if we got caught on the ground, they'd set the dogs off, when the only protection we'd have was our great-coats. We never really slept, which meant we were always on edge. We could see helicopters up above, spotlights, and hear the troops. And they were all utterly focused on capturing a potential Special Forces soldier. And even if we couldn't actually see or hear anything, we thought we could.

* * *

Before being released back onto the hills, the DS threw a big party for the locals, with loads of food and booze. At this party, they had pictures of all the recruits up on a wall underneath a sign that said, 'If you see any of these people, call this number'. The locals were told that we weren't allowed to have any civilian contact, that they weren't allowed to give us shelter and to let our bosses know if they found us in any of their barns. But the locals did the exact opposite. Having been plied with food and booze at the party, they'd go straight to the supermarket, get stocked up on provisions, and wait for a knock on the door from a bedraggled and desperate recruit.

The locals were like the resistance, and most people who have passed Selection have used their initiative and used the resistance at some point. Even the DS know it's happening, because they went through the same process. Ultimately, it's about not getting caught 'cheating'. Because if it happens for real, getting caught means you'll probably get killed.

We were soon so cold that we couldn't feel our feet, so we decided to find a barn and get some heat back into us. While we were lying on top of hay bales, working in pairs, trying to warm up our feet in each other's armpits, one of the lads suddenly said, 'Shall we try to see if anyone's in the farmhouse?' To begin with, everyone said no. But then we all started thinking how lovely it would be to be toasting in front of an open hearth, while tucked up under a duvet. Soon enough, one of the lads was knocking on the farmer's door and the farmer was in the barn, telling us all to follow him into the house.

The farmer had a roaring fire almost up to the ceiling and his missus was pottering about in a pinny in the kitchen, whipping up a roast. If there is a heaven, this is what it must look like. Thawed out, we got as much food into us as humanly possible, lay down by the fire and fell into a gloriously deep sleep.

When we woke up, we discovered the farmer had decided to go to the local pub. When he returned, he was shitfaced and started shouting, 'Lads, I'll give you a lift to wherever you need to be!'

'There's no way we're getting in a car with you.'

'Don't worry, I've got my handyman with me, he's gonna drive!'

'Mate, we're still not getting in that car, no way...'

A few hours later, after grabbing more precious sleep, we were squeezed into the back of the farmer's car and on our way. As we approached the RV, we could see helicopters hovering above and spotlights getting closer and closer. The handyman stopped at the bottom of a hill, but when we tried to open the car doors, we couldn't. We had to move quick, so were frantic. Suddenly, the farmer climbed out of the car and started shouting, 'I'll give you a hand, lads, it's a bit of a sticky door...' The next thing I heard was a loud thud, which I thought was the front door being closed heavy-handedly. Meanwhile, one of the lads had kicked a door open, so we all piled out and ran into the woods.

A couple of days later, as we moved in on our RV, we could see a couple of familiar DS manning the checkpoint. We knew something was up, because it was usually someone we'd never met. One of the DSs told me to get the rest of the patrol, I gathered them up and as soon as we were taken in, the training officer started firing questions at us: 'Where have you been? What have you been up to? Do you know this farmer? Or his wife Mildred? Or Barney his dog? Arthur the cat? Daisy the cow?' I was sitting there thinking, 'Shit! We've been busted, we have to come clean...'

In the end, we told them everything that had happened, and the training officer said, 'Right, you're done.' Apparently, the farmer had fallen over – hence the loud thud – and banged his head on the pavement. At the hospital, he'd told them that he'd been beaten up by the SAS. I don't know why, maybe he was trying to get some compensation. The police then relayed his story back to the DS, we'd been turfed out, and now we were being returned to unit.

I had visualised the end a thousand times, what it would look and feel like. In my mind, I was already living in my own house in Poole. I could even see my name on my locker. I was in the Special Boat Service. It was done. But in that moment, everything I'd dreamed about, everything I'd worked so hard for, went up in smoke. All that graft, all that hardship, for nothing. There were no tears, but it was the lowest I'd ever felt. I was in a state of shock. Surely there had been some kind of mistake? This can't be the end? For the first few days, I kept waiting for someone to pull me in and say, 'Actually, the farmer has retracted his story.' But it never happened. My fate was non-negotiable.

Mum was very supportive, as she always was, but what was anyone supposed to say? 'Oh well, more fool them, there are plenty of other similar jobs out there.' This wasn't a normal job interview, this was seven months of hell with a 5 per cent pass rate. And I'd been one of the few. People dream of being in that situation, and I'd not failed because of my lack of fitness or mental strength, I'd failed because some pissed-up bastard had grassed me up.

But I didn't feel bitter towards the training team for failing me. I didn't even feel bitter towards the farmer. The overwhelming feeling was that of embarrassment. Nobody says, 'But look at how well you did, up until the point you failed.' The journey doesn't matter to the outside world. All that matters is the outcome: did I achieve my goal? I didn't, and that was the bottom line.

6

MUMMY'S BOY

As soon as I got into remand home, I was stripped down to nothing, literally and metaphorically. I was put in the same clothes as everyone else, which was horrible for me. I'd always wanted to be an individual and now I was no different to all the other idiots who'd landed themselves in there. My mum came to see me and she was, unsurprisingly, distraught. Her son's life was disintegrating before her eyes and it seemed clear that I was going to be sent down. My brother had been implicated but I got pushed forward as the sacrificial lamb, because my dad didn't want both his boys in the shit. My brother was older, I didn't have to persuade him to do anything, and looking back I realise how severe it was that I had to take all the blame.

There was a lot of dodgy stuff going on in that remand home. The closest thing I can compare it to is joining up with the Marines, which doesn't reflect very well on the military in this country. Not long after arriving, the remand home 'daddy' headbutted me and every day after that I was told I was going to be 'DBd', which meant I was going to be the recipient of a dorm battering. For some reason, that never happened. But one night I woke up to see a load of kids standing over a bed, masturbating and flicking semen over this sleeping boy's face. Years later, the police interviewed me about my time there, because there had been a lot of sexual abuse allegations against staff. I was

only there for a short time, so for them to come to me suggests
it was rife.

Two weeks after being locked up, I was taken off for trial.
Seeing my mates again was awesome, like a brotherhood reuniting.
There were four of us sitting in the dock, along this leather Ches-
terfield-style bench with buttons on. My mum was in court, in
floods of tears. She thought I wasn't coming home for a long time.

The judge came in, told us all to rise and said his piece. And
when we all sat down again, a load of buttons pinged off the
bench. I didn't really give a shit about what was happening,
because I thought I was going down and that was the end of
it. So when I saw these buttons go flying, I dissolved into fits of
laughter. All four of us were in bits, heads in hands, shoulders
rolling, tears streaming down our cheeks, letting out little snorts
and squeaks.

We managed to get a grip before they read our charge sheets,
and my charge was way beyond anyone else's. As it was being
relayed to the court, my mum fell into the throes of a second wave
of grief. I was rather more accepting of the whole situation, you
might even say laid-back. But, astonishingly, they decided not to
send me down. Instead, I got two years' conditional discharge,
two years' supervision and lots of other stuff I didn't understand.

Afterwards, our lawyer said to us, 'I have no idea how you
didn't get sent down. I think the judge showed leniency because
you were all crying when you first came in...' Crying! We were
laughing our tits off! Thank God for that bench and those faulty
buttons. Apart from the supposed crying, psychiatric reports were
produced in court, which showed that my father had left, my
grandparents had recently died, and I was suffering from a lack
of attention. Whatever the reasons for the leniency, I had dodged
another bullet.

That whole episode with the shotgun was a wake-up call. Thank God for the Mitchell sister and her loose lips. I needed, and subconsciously wanted, someone to put a hand on my shoulder and stop me going down the wrong path. I didn't even recognise that I was playing with fire, but there was a voice deep inside of me screaming, 'Please, someone stop me!' Until that happened, I was going to push and push and push myself down the wrong path. But from that moment on, my long-suffering mum – whose whole world had fallen apart, who was broke, emotionally and financially – led me from the darkness and into the light.

My mum was an angel, almost faultless. I was very much a mother's boy. I idolised her from an early age and she showered me with love and affection. And when I needed direction most, she was the person who put her hand on my shoulder to guide me where I needed to go.

When you're a kid, you don't understand or really care what your parents are feeling. I never knew there were problems going on between Mum and Dad, she always seemed quite unaffected by anything. And even after my dad left and my mum was going through terrible hardship – grieving for the loss of her parents, with three mouths to feed, no help from my dad and a son who was spiralling out of control – she soldiered on without complaint.

Mum wasn't the kind of woman who cared about keeping up appearances. My dad would have been extremely embarrassed about my brushes with the law, but my mum didn't give a shit what anyone outside of the family thought. Nothing else mattered apart from me and my brother and sister, and all she wanted to do was wrap her arms around the family and pull them closer. She even saw the funny side eventually, just as she manages to see the funny side in almost anything.

Although she never forgave my dad for leaving us in the lurch, it didn't take Mum too long to realise that my dad leaving was best for everyone, including her. She started scuba diving. She fell in with a young crowd and would throw these great parties at the house, with lots of drinking, singing and dancing. This was a woman who had wanted to join the Navy, so she had this pent-up sense of adventure. It was still hard for her financially and practically, with three kids to look after, but she had a new lease of life. It felt like the black clouds had scuttled off and suddenly there was a lot of fun to be had in the house.

Mum went out with a few blokes her age and found them boring, or we drove them out. For a while she was seeing this very well-to-do guy with a double-barrelled name, and he ended up leaving because we were just too wild. Eventually, Mum started seeing a bloke called Simon who was 20 when she was in her late thirties and I was 15. She'd just picked us up from somewhere when she pulled over and said, 'Look, I'm seeing someone else. And he's quite young...' She was apprehensive about telling us, but we didn't bat an eyelid. We were just happy that Mum was happy. And this new guy had a foot in both camps: he could hang out with Mum and also hang out with us. It wasn't just a phase Mum was going through, either, because she ended up marrying Simon and they're still together and extremely happy.

My brother and I had go-karts, which we'd bomb around in over the playing fields. The police came over one day – again – because someone had reported us for go-karting on recreation land. We were hiding at the top of the stairs and could hear Mum saying, 'Those little buggers, I keep telling them not to do this. Boys! Where are you?' She came marching down the corridor, pretending to look for us, and we were on the landing laughing our heads off.

Eventually, she went back to the police and said, 'Look, I don't know where they are, but I'll make sure they get a good telling off.' That was good enough for the police. What Mum hadn't seemed to appreciate were the two muddy tyre tracks all the way up her back and the grass in her hair. At times, Mum was as mischievous as us.

She encouraged me with everything I showed an interest in. I was a decent runner, so she ferried me to cross-country races at weekends and was always watching when I was competing on the track in the 1500 metres. My best mate Mark Sheriff was a brilliant runner and we raced together. But I got kicked out of the athletics club because I wouldn't train. I was one of those kids who rocked up for a race and smashed it. I just couldn't be bothered, had too many other things going on and couldn't dedicate myself to one thing. But at least I had positive things going on in my life, activities that gave my existence a meaningful purpose and made me feel vibrant and worthwhile.

Not that my path was entirely straight and narrow after the shotgun incident. Unexpectedly, I was chosen to be Yellow Team's sports day captain by my classmates, which was actually quite a proud moment. But because of the trouble I'd been in, the teachers put the kybosh on it. That rejection was a massive blow to me. It made me hate school even more and I resented everything about it after that. True, I was a pain in the arse at times and failed just about everything academic. But they turned their back on me after the shotgun incident, weren't prepared to encourage any growth or entertain the idea that I might be able to recover the situation and make good. As far as they were concerned, I was a lost cause and a terrible influence.

I had this rivalry with another kid in the 1500 metres, and our race at sports day was supposed to be a life-and-death battle.

I hadn't trained and this other kid was the favourite, but I wiped the floor with him, beat him by about 200 metres. After crossing the finish line, I walked straight off the track rather than sticking around for prize giving. I didn't look back, and all the while I was thinking, 'Fuck you all...'

After the shotgun incident, I became a bit of a loner. The kids from my school decided I was a nutter and their parents were probably telling them to stay away from me. I picked mates from a different school, and they included some of the hardest families in town. I started drinking, going out to pubs and clubs, back when you could get in pretty much anywhere at the age of 15. Not that drinking was unheard of in my family. In Burton, a lot of people worked in the brewery industry and used to get paid in beer. My mum worked in a managerial role at a brewery; my brother did an apprenticeship as an electrician and went to work at a brewery; my sister worked for a brewery and would come home with crates of Diamond White stacked up in her car boot.

I started skiving off even more, so when my dad invited me over to Malta, where he was selling timeshares, I jumped at the chance. The plan was for me to revise for GCSEs while I was staying with my dad for a couple of weeks, but I never bothered finding out when my exams were. When my classmates were revising, I was sunbathing on a beach. I returned from Malta with my hair bleached white and this amazing tan, but I'd missed most of my exams. I was walking down the corridor at school when someone ran up to me and said, 'Fucking hell, Ollie, Mr Henry's after you, he's hunting you down!' I just thought, 'Fuck this', walked out of the school and never went back.

My dad disowned me for a second time, but I didn't give a shit. I didn't see any value in the education system, had no interest. I didn't have any bandwidth left to absorb any pointless knowledge, there was so much else going on in my head. I was joining the Marines, and that was that. Nothing else mattered.

* * *

Kids who are constantly getting into trouble don't normally have their hearts set on joining the military. It doesn't really add up, because if they're rebelling against institutions and authority, the last place they want to be is in the Army, being shouted at and told what to do every minute of every day. I know my mum was surprised, because she knew only too well how wild I was. The first time I was put on report at school, I came home, handed my mum a piece of paper, she opened it up and looked aghast. On the piece of paper, a teacher had written: 'I received this report card in the form of a paper aeroplane.'

The teachers used to say I could attain so much if I wanted to. But I didn't. But even though I was out of control, I craved stability and responsibility. Being a kid wasn't enough for me. I wanted to be a man already. My mum said to me, 'Matthew, how are you going to be a Marine if you can't take orders?'

And I replied, 'The Marines will be different, because everyone else will be doing the same.'

I wanted to join when I was 16, but was advised to wait until I was 18, otherwise my criminal convictions would have appeared on my military record. While I was on probation, my mum would drive me to Derby every week, where we'd visit the Royal Navy Marines careers office. Apart from the lady who scoffed at the idea of me piloting a submersible insertion craft, they were great to me. They'd talk to me for ages, let me read magazines and watch the training videos. Although I do remember my mum asking an officer what they'd teach me as a trade, and the officer replying: 'To kill.' My mum tells me she wanted to cry.

For two years I was in limbo, doing manual labour jobs to tide me over. Having started talking to my dad again, I even worked for him selling timeshares. I was one of those annoying people on the seafront, bothering you when you just want to have a nice stroll and eat an ice cream. I lasted two days before jacking it in. I didn't stick at anything, because I didn't have a passion for anything. Whether it was school, digging holes or flogging timeshares, none of it made me feel like I was living.

7

THE WIDEST SMILE

never heard anything about the situation with the farmer again, it was all just dusted under the carpet. Clearly, the DS had decided that his story was a load of bollocks, otherwise they would have taken further action. But the fact of the matter was, I'd jumped in a car with a pisshead and compromised myself.

You are allowed two goes at Selection, so I had the option of giving it one more crack. But that wasn't my immediate thought when I got back to 45 Commando. It wasn't that I was embarrassed at having to return. Most Royal Marines are very conscious of their limitations, as most people are. They are crack soldiers just by virtue of being Royal Marines, but most don't think they've got it in them to even apply for Special Forces Selection. So there was huge admiration and support for how far I'd got. But I'd started to doubt my military career all over again.

Selection takes almost everything out of you, strips you back to your bare minimum, physically and mentally, before asking the question, 'Now, what have you got?' You end up reaching deep inside yourself, trying to dredge up every last grain of resolve. It's about seeing if you've got the necessary minerals to find something in those lowest moments, for example, if you're captured behind enemy lines or retreating and being hunted down like rats.

I'd gone from almost leaving to almost getting into the Special Forces to being sent back to a place I had been desperate to escape from, a place I thought I'd never see again. It was almost like being recaptured, and the idea of having to do it all again didn't seem that appealing. But I soon came to my senses. The fact I'd come so close once gave me the energy to do it all over again. On top of that, I could still remember the words of my sergeant ('This is going to be hilarious!') and I still had this flickering passion to be a Special Forces operator. Soon those flickers were fanned into a raging fire again.

Second time around, SAS and SBS Selections had amalgamated, so that there were 250 of us at pre-selection in Hereford and it was only at the very end that people would be separated. In fact, I'm one of only a couple of people who have done SAS and SBS Selection, in its previous form. Amalgamation meant I'd have to tackle the dreaded Hills Phase, so this was going to be new ground. We'd be out on those hills day after day, running, marching, covering large distances in a limited amount of time, all while carrying a Bergen and a rifle. And it wasn't just aimless yomping, we were having to navigate, reach checkpoints, and all without any direction or encouragement from the DS. And if I suffered a bad injury or failed a march, that was it.

But the early signs were good. We lost so many people on that first march over the Pen y Fan, the highest peak on the Brecon Beacons. After day one, as many as 20 per cent of the recruits were on their way home. But I smashed it. We had to cover 26 kilometres in under four hours and I was one of the first five or six home.

What I found odd about the Hills Phase was that we had an agenda, so we knew everything we were going to be doing. When it was purely SBS, we didn't know our arses from our elbows and survived on next to no sleep for the duration, and that was the hardest part. So the first two weeks was nothing compared to what I'd already been through. After day one, I was lying in bed thinking, 'It can't be as simple as this.' I was waiting for someone to burst into the room and throw a flash-crash distraction device at me. But, mercifully, it never happened.

But about three days in, I was coming towards the end of a march and among the first five or six again when disaster struck. I was carrying quite a heavy load, it was raining and wet under foot. As I made my way down this track towards the finish, pushing harder than was probably sensible, a slate slid under my foot. My ankle went over 90 degrees and I could feel and hear the tendons snapping. It wasn't pain that I was in, it was a state of shock: 'I've just fucked myself again. And this time, I'm not going to get another chance.'

I hobbled to the end and went straight to the medic, who helped me take my boot off. My ankle already resembled a balloon. The medic looked at a DS and slid a finger across his throat, meaning that he thought I was finished. Meanwhile, I was thinking, 'Why is he doing that? Fuck, they think I'm dead.'

Back in camp that evening, the training officer who had failed me the first time called me in and said, 'Right, we've seen the state of your ankle, I've spoken to the medics and we're going to give you a medical withdrawal, which means you can come back and try again. If you try to carry on and fail a march, you're gone and can never come back.'

The training officer thought my response was a foregone conclusion. But I replied, 'With all due respect, sir, I'm not prepared to go home.' As far as I was concerned, this was it. I didn't have the will to return to 45 Commando. If I accepted the medical withdrawal, I'd never go back.

The training officer shook his head in disbelief and said, 'Man up! Take the medical withdrawal and come back when you're fit.'

'No!'

'Well, as far as I'm concerned, you've failed. And it's your own fucking fault.'

I turned around and hopped out of the office.

In Selection, people are looking for the first excuse to bail out. You'll see people dropping out with twisted knees and ankles, blisters and bad backs. They're looking for something physical to blame because the alternative is to say, 'I couldn't handle it mentally, so I had to throw in the towel.' I didn't want to be one of those people, even though my injury was worse than anyone's I'd seen that had withdrawn before that point.

The following morning, I got up early, strapped up my ankle with reams and reams of medical tape and swallowed a shitload of ibuprofen. At the start of that day's march, the DS were looking at me with disappointed faces, probably thinking, 'What an idiot. And what a fucking waste.'

The march was across the Elan Valley, which is some of the most frustrating, ankle bending terrain in Special Forces Selection. The Elan Valley is a green, marshy desert, with leg-sapping peat bogs and football-sized tufts of grass known as babies' heads. More people are failed or voluntarily withdraw on the Elan Valley marches than any other. And, just as I suspected, it was fucking horrendous. Throughout the march, I had tears streaming down my cheeks from the pain. I just scraped through, but I had another week to go.

But that's just what I kept doing every day: guzzling pain-killers, deleting some of the pain, listening to the Neneh Cherry song '7 Seconds' over and over in my head (it must have been on the radio a lot at the time!) and doing just enough not to get red carded. That was down to pure desire. I just wasn't prepared to go home. I'd visualised how things would pan out and I used that as my focus. Although towards the end, I had to shelve that vision, because it would have become too overwhelming. When things get really tough, you have to boil it down to getting one foot in front of the other.

It might sound horrible, but seeing people fall by the wayside massively boosts your own confidence. I sometimes laugh about it with Jason Fox, my old colleague and mate from *SAS: Who Dares Wins*. We refer to it as 'the Quickening', that phenomenon from the film *Highlander* when a character chops an enemy's head off and steals all their energy.

Up in the hills, I'd see older, more experienced, stronger-looking people dropping to their knees, crying and puking their guts up. And as I went past, I'd almost be able to see inside them. They'd be completely hollowed out, empty, with nothing left. Sometimes I'd say, 'Mate, come on let's do this together!' As soon as it was clear that they were going no further, I knew their remaining energy was on offer. They'd grimace and nod and I'd get this injection of power, like a lightning bolt of electricity, before disappearing into the distance.

Selection was the one place I'd been where image didn't mean anything. Humans are always self-doubting, always looking for things to go wrong. But Selection made me realise how debilitating that thought process is. Our idea of where our limits are is often misjudged, because we're constantly comparing ourselves unfavourably to others. But it didn't matter how big or strong or fit someone looked before the start of Selection, it was all just perception.

That's why you don't just pick the fittest people and be done with it, because you can put the fittest person in the world behind enemy lines and they might crumble under the mental pressure. Selection doesn't care if you can run a marathon in under two-and-a-half hours or you compete in Iron Man triathlons every other weekend. Far more important is that you can endure a high degree of mental discomfort for extended periods of time.

The DS just couldn't get their heads around how I was managing to continue. The tutting and head-shaking was replaced by raised eyebrows and wry smiles. And then, after the first week, the pain started to plateau. I'd seen off the worst, or at least learned to accept it.

I don't blame the DS for doubting me. In fact, he was a good egg to have offered me that medical withdrawal. The DS clearly thought I had it in me to be a Special Forces soldier and didn't want to see me throw away the opportunity. But people doubting you can be such a powerful motivation, especially once you realise that a lot of people who doubt you are doubting themselves. Seeing other people push themselves to the limit and achieve outlandish things is horrible for some people. They know, often deep inside, that if they really, really tried, they could do what you're doing. But there's something stopping them from taking that first step. Once you've done that, the other foot naturally follows.

A huge number of recruits didn't make it through the Hills Phase. But I did, and I earned a lot of respect from the DS for doing so. Not that they were popping champagne and showering me with kisses. It was more a case of, 'Fuck off home, I'll see you next week.'

My ankle still wasn't what it should have been, but it had come a long way. And, of course, I had been in the jungle before. One of my DS was a guy who was captured during the famous Bravo Two Zero exfiltration in the First Gulf War, later immortalised by Andy McNab in his book of the same name. This guy was a legend to all the lads, so I was desperate to impress him. Whenever our patrol got lost, he'd say, 'Ollie, tell us where we are.' And I'd usually be able to, because I had wealth of experience after completing this phase before. But a week or so in, a DS decided to give me a bit of a buzz. He came up behind me and said, 'How long do you think you'll end up doing?'

'What do you mean?'

'Well, how long do you think you'll last in the jungle?'

'I'll do it all, I hope...'

After that brief exchange, the DS walked off. I thought, 'Fuck, what was that all about?' I thought I'd been doing brilliantly, but now I wasn't so sure.

From when you're a kid, you're always looking for validation. When you're at school, you'll draw a picture, take it home so your mum can ruffle your hair and say, 'Oh, what a wonderful drawing. I'm going to stick it on the fridge so that everyone can see it.' Whatever you do, you want someone to put their arm around you and tell you how well you did it. You expect praise from teachers, university lecturers, colleagues and bosses. When a footballer scores a goal, he expects cuddles from his teammates and a thumbs-up from the boss, not to mention the cheers of thousands of supporters. When a guitarist finishes a solo, he expects a smile and a wink from his bandmate, the crowd to go wild, and a groupie or two secured in his trailer post-concert. But Selection gives you none of that. And until you've had that validation taken away, you don't realise the dependency it creates.

In Special Forces training, you might be smashing every march, nailing all the skills and feeling like a first-class Special Forces soldier in the making, but if nobody is telling you that, the worm of doubt wriggles its way into your mind and starts eating away at you. That lack of validation can rot you from the inside. People fail themselves in the jungle. Before they know it, self-doubt has consumed them. Their concentration goes awry, they start making mistakes doing weapons skills, stop attending to personal admin.

And here's the kicker: while it feels like nobody is playing a blind bit of notice to what you're doing, you're actually being watched at all times, because the DS send out local trackers to trail the patrols. These guys, who are able to smell body odour, shit, urine and toothpaste from 100 metres away, study everything you do, and any sub-standard soldiering is reported back to the DS. When the DS discuss a recruit, everything boils down to one question: would you want that soldier to be working by your side in a few months' time?

Discovering you're being observed and judged without you noticing can be very unnerving. But at least it flushes out some of the 'DS watchers', those recruits who look like Superman whenever the assessors are around but start to shirk whenever they're not. I saw a lot of those guys during the Hills Phase. They tended not to last very long in the jungle, with its all-seeing eyes.

Selection is about conquering your own mind. To do that, you have to learn to self-validate, which might simply mean telling yourself you've had a good day when you've got a bit of time on your hands. Because in a real combat situation, you're not going to have someone patting you on the back and saying, 'Well done! Great shooting. Would you like a hug?'

One morning in the jungle, I was told to make my way to the helicopter landing site. When I got there, the training officer was standing in the middle. My immediate thought was, 'Fuck. Is this the end? Have I failed again?'

The officer said, 'Do you know why you're here?'

'No.'

'Do you think you've done all right so far?'

'Yeah, I think I've done everything I've been asked to do.'

'Well done, we've seen enough.'

That was that. I don't think they were doing it out of the kindness of their hearts, I think they probably thought that because I'd been there before, I was being more helpful to my patrol than they were comfortable with.

The helicopter came down, I jumped on to the outer skids and suddenly I was flying over the vast sea of broccoli, my whoops and hollers drowned out by the sound of the rotors. I spent the next two weeks sunbathing on the beach, catching stingray and supping beer. But not everyone had such a beautiful homecoming. Some were taken into a room and told that they'd failed. A lot of lads get binned at that point, which must be like making it through a 12-round title fight and losing on points. The bad news leaves a lot of very tough lads in floods of tears. But I wasn't too worried. I had the widest smile of all.

8

SPECIAL, AT LAST

efore I got to Hereford for my second round of skills training, I split up with Helen for a short while. So I was single, had nothing to worry about and was absolutely loving it. One Saturday, I decided to round the lads up for a night on the razzle. The plan was to get haircuts, buy some new clobber, have a bit of lunch, hit the town, sink some beers and hopefully still be able to talk to some women.

Hair done, we headed to the shops. Most of the lads disappeared into Top Man or Next, but I was more into Armani and Gucci, so me and two lads called Zak and Chaz made our way to a boutique that sold all the top gear. I was flicking through the shirts, when all of a sudden I heard this scuffle. When I turned around, I saw the shop owner bent over and pulling up Chaz's trouser leg, revealing a pair of jeans underneath. Ring any bells? Yep, this is exactly what I got nicked for when I was an out-of-control teenager. Back then, I thought I was a genius for thinking of it, as if I'd invented fire. Until the police told me it was one of the oldest tricks in the book and what an idiot I'd been.

My mate managed to kick the shop owner off and legged it, before the shop owner closed the door, locked it and said to me, 'You're not going anywhere...' I'd been minding my own business, so I wasn't having any of it. But when I tried to walk past her, she started wrestling with me. Before I knew it, we'd toppled over, taken out a mannequin and fallen into the window. Imagine if you'd been window shopping in Hereford that day. And the town was mobbed with weekend shoppers.

I managed to push her off and get through the door, before screaming down the street to the local car park. Heading back to Stirling Lines garrison, I couldn't believe what had just happened. There was a helicopter buzzing overhead and I was thinking, 'Fucking hell, they've scrambled a chopper to search for me.' All sorts of crazy possibilities were going through my head. And the fact I'd done nothing wrong did nothing to allay my fears, because rolling about on the floor with a female shop owner and a mannequin is not a good look.

I managed to get myself back to the garrison without being captured, and when I walked into the dorm, Zak and Chaz were sitting there smirking. Suffice to say, I didn't find the situation as amusing as they did.

'You fucking idiots! What the fuck have you just done?'

'Oh, we'll be all right. Who's gonna find out?'

As they were saying that, an MOD police car came down the drive.

'Whatever happens, I was not involved with this. You'd better tell the police the truth.'

It transpired that Zak had told Chaz about this genius shop-lifting trick and Chaz, thinking it was this brand-new wheeze, had gone and done what he was told. The fucking morons had been planning it the whole time, as if it was the Great Train Robbery and they were Ronnie Biggs and Buster Edwards.

We were taken down to the police cells and it all erupted. I told the police that it was fuck all to do with me and suggested that they talk to the shop owner. Even that suggestion carried an element of risk, because even though it was true that I didn't try to nick anything, I did end up wrestling with her and one of her mannequins in the shop window. Meanwhile, Chaz had confessed, but Zak had denied knowing anything about it.

The rest of that weekend was hideous. Having been falsely accused of beating someone up, I now thought I was going to be binned because my mate had tried to nick a pair of jeans. As funny as it sounds, at the time I genuinely thought they were going to chuck me out in disgrace for a second time, never to return. On the Monday morning, the same DS who had thrown me off the first time popped up again to rip me a new arsehole. And the whole time he was bollocking me, I just felt so embarrassed. I knew exactly how pathetic the situation was, because I'd done it myself as a dumb 14-year-old kid.

I pleaded with the DS to speak to the civilian police, but he wasn't interested. As far as my bosses were concerned, an unsavoury incident had taken place and even if I had nothing to do with it, I was with the miscreants when it happened. As it turned out, Zak got away with it, but Chaz got dumped and sent back to the Marines. That was such a shame, because he was such a great bloke. I felt so sorry for him and I still speak to him today. For the rest of his life, he'll have to tell people that he very nearly became a member of the Special Forces but got thrown out at the last minute for trying to lift a pair of jeans. As for me, I remained on the course by the skin of my teeth.

Soldiers have a self-destructive streak, there is no doubt about it. Chaz had gone through months of hell, had one foot in the door of the most illustrious fighting force in the world, and he risked it all for a short-term thrill. No rational person would do that. A lot of soldiers tell me they want to tear their lives down and start again. Soldiers have this ordered world created for us and all we want to do is pull the pin, blow it apart and deal with the chaos.

It sounds like madness, but it's that borderline madness that gets soldiers into the Special Forces. And it also makes perfect sense, because soldiers sit happily amid chaos. It's as natural as a bird sitting in a tree.

After the Not-So-Great Boutique Robbery, there were all kinds of jokes going around: What's the difference between the SBS and the SAS? It's all in the jeans… I was just embarrassed that I'd been a part of it.

Second time being hunted down on the hills was pretty much the same as before, except I was that little bit wiser. Before we were released, I got some 20-pound notes, screwed them up as tightly as possible, put them inside some condoms and swallowed them, knowing that in two or three days' time I'd shit them out. And having advised the rest of the patrol to do the same, we'd be loaded. I've heard stories about people swallowing all sorts, even watches.

Even after my experience the first time, I still believed in accessing barns and houses whenever we could. One day, we took shelter in this derelict house and shit out some money, like some weird, human ATMs. We had 40 quid between us, so the next step was to find a shop where we could spend it.

I discovered some workers' clothes, put them on and hitch-hiked to the local village, where I found a mini-mart. I filled a basket with Mars bars, crisps and cans of Coke and was dropping the basket on the counter when I heard someone say, 'The boys have turned up.' I looked to my right and saw a troop carrier from Hunter Force pulling up outside. Oh. My. Fucking. God.

These boys had pictures of us, so I was shitting myself. They started filing into the shop and I was standing there with my 100 Mars bars trying not to talk, because I didn't want anyone to know I was English. When the girl behind the counter asked how my day had been, I mumbled something incomprehensible under my breath.

I settled up, put my head down and waved some soldiers in as I left. When I walked past the troop carrier, they were all looking out of the back, looking hard as fuck and no doubt thinking, 'Look at that soft civilian prick...'

When I got back to the house, I was handing out the grub and telling the other lads about my close shave when someone shouted, 'Fuck! There's a patrol coming down the street!' Most of the lads hid, but I was still in my overalls and by this time a couple of builders had turned up. So I said to them, 'What can I do to help?' When the soldiers arrived, looking menacing with their guns, I was shoveling cement into a mixer. I pushed it further and shouted in my best Welsh accent, 'All right, boys?' The soldiers smiled, waved back and off they trotted.

Second time around, I made it through the escape exercises without being accused of punching a farmer. The end came after ten days on the run, when we reached an RV and people suddenly came at us from all angles. That was when we knew the 'harshing' had begun. We were bundled into a cattle truck, driven off to an unspecified destination and when we were bundled off again, there was a lot of jostling and screaming and shouting, as well as dogs roaming around us, growling and foaming at the mouth.

As I stood there, two guys worked their way around me, prodding and poking and talking right in my ear. It was as if they were performing a weird comedy act, or they were grotesque clowns from a horror film. One of them kept pushing me and saying, 'Look at him! Look at him!' in this creepy high-pitched voice. It was very unsettling. Which, of course, it was meant to be.

The clowns were the warm-up act for 36 hours of interrogation, which began with being hooded and led out onto a shale-covered area. Then they turned the stereo on. Unfortunately, the speakers weren't playing my favourite tunes, they were pumping out this horrendous white noise. Imagine the sound you hear when you phone a fax machine by mistake, mingled with hundreds of nails being scraped down a blackboard, except 100 times louder, and you'll get the idea. While they were attempting to make our ears bleed and our brains melt, they were putting us into various stress positions. Every time I lost my shape, someone would stick their knee between my shoulders or pull my elbows back. There always seemed to be a person hovering over me. This lasted for a good few hours, before they took us away for questioning.

Having given me a boiler suit to wear, they pushed me into a room and stripped me naked. I still had my hood on but could feel someone moving around me. Without warning, the hood was removed to reveal three women sitting behind a desk. Suddenly, one of them started pointing at my cock and shouting, 'What the fuck is that?' For what seemed like hours, they were taking the piss out of me, telling me how pathetic I was and laughing. Between the abuse and the demoralisation, they kept asking me for my name, rank and number, the point being that I wasn't allowed to give it to them. There is one thing I should say before we move on: it was very cold in that room...

Suddenly, I was strapped naked to a pallet and they were hosing me down with freezing water. And the whole time that was happening, I wished I was back in interrogation. I just couldn't wait for it to end. But when they started interrogating you again, you wished you were being hosed down with freezing water. In another room, there was this big bloke sitting behind a desk with a bag of sweets on it. Over and over again, he'd ask me for my name, rank and number, between popping sweets into his mouth. In another room, there was a really nice guy, whose whole purpose was to put you at ease and catch you off guard. You've got to avoid saying yes or no in interrogation, and the nice guy was the interrogator most likely to make you forget yourself.

When you first go in for interrogation, you know you've got 36 hours of it. But you have to forget all about the goal and measure the time in seconds. You can almost feel your brain frying, so that sometimes you don't know what you're doing or saying. You just have to hope that while you're on autopilot, you're not doing or saying anything wrong. It's full-on psychological warfare, the weirdest thing I've ever experienced. The games they play are vicious and cruel. It reminded me of that scene in the film *A Clockwork Orange*, when they clamp the main character's eyes open, experiment on him and torture him with Beethoven's Ninth Symphony. And it certainly gave me an insight into how horrendous it must be for people who are taken hostage for real.

Most make it through interrogation, but some people fall down the home straight. One of them was Zak, who was suddenly singing like a canary. He was telling his interrogators about security at our base, that he could get access to the CCTV systems, and just about everything else he shouldn't have been. Afterwards, a rumour went round that he was given a truth serum. I've got no idea if that was true, but the story went that they wanted him off because of the incident with the jeans. And why on earth would he be telling them that stuff otherwise? It just didn't make any sense. Either way, I didn't give a fuck, given that he'd messed up everything for my mate Chaz.

When the 36 hours were up, I was taken into a room, my hood was removed and there was an officer standing in front of me. Without any fanfare, he said, 'I am the umpire. You've passed. Congratulations.' There was no cinematic moment where I was whooping and hollering and high-fiving the umpire, but it did feel like a boulder had just rolled off my shoulders. Out of 250 soldiers who began Selection, I was one of only seven who made it to the end. I was 23 years old and a member of the illustrious Special Boat Service. My old maths teacher might have been surprised if he ever found out. I wasn't.

9

RATHER BEAUTIFUL

Even to this day, my mum says to me: 'I phone your brother, he tells me what's going on with his life and I nod and say, "Oh, that's very nice." I phone your sister and it's much the same. Then I phone you, you tell me what's going on and when I put down the phone I think to myself, "That boy's life..."' The thought of my mum telling her friends what I'm up to makes me giggle, because I know they'll be raising their eyebrows and scratching their heads.

Whether it was fighting off apes in a circus, firing stolen shotguns over people's heads, jumping off harbour walls at the age of three or abseiling down buildings, my life had always been a bit different. And I wouldn't have it any other way. I see young lads setting off on their career path, which will involve sitting in an office for five days a week, for the next 40-odd years, and think: 'Is that really what you're going to do for the rest of your lives?' They start earning decent money, get a mortgage and, before they know it, they're stuck in a rut.

Through my business, I meet older guys from the corporate world and they'll say to me, 'I can't fucking believe I'm still doing the same job. I just feel so lost. But because it provides me and my family with a certain lifestyle, I can't escape it.' I don't know how people exist like that, because it means they're destined never to achieve anything that will give their lives meaning.

The majority prefer to take the well-trodden path, rather than the path less travelled, because taking the path less travelled means having to hack your way through. That's a difficult thing to do – or at least it seems difficult, when you're standing staring at the overgrowth and you don't even have a machete.

Some people need to know exactly what their future will be and become lost in society's perception of what happiness is supposed to look like. Owning nice houses and expensive cars and watches is a way of justifying their existence. But how many times does cooking in your 50-grand kitchen, climbing into your 100-grand Porsche or looking at your 10-grand Rolex watch actually make you happy? For the first week, maybe? After that, not much.

Everyone is beset by fear and negativity. It's fear and negativity that has kept us alive since the dawn of time. All of us are living in the repeat cycle of yesterday, our minds tailored to a survival pattern. That means doing the same today as we did yesterday and every day before that, because that's what has kept us alive until now. It doesn't matter if we've been sad and unfulfilled for as long as we can remember, all we focus on is the fact that we're still here.

That's why people find it so difficult to break out of the cycle. And even if someone does manage to break out, their brain starts saying, 'No, this is too scary, this is too difficult, you need to get back into your comfort zone.' But the notion of comfort zones is contradictory. Living life in a comfort zone might feel comfortable, but it's just existing. It's like living your life in a trench. There might be water up to your knees and rats running around your ankles and you might be miserable as hell. But as soon as you pluck up the courage to stick your head over the top, bullets start firing and you think, 'Fuck this, I'm getting back in...' The mind is devious. Whether it's thinking about going to the gym or quitting the job you hate, it will come up with all these different reasons why you're better off where you are, back in that horrible trench.

I hate social conformity with a passion. I see so many people conforming, people who don't even know why they're doing what they're doing. If you asked them why, they wouldn't have a clue. That's such a waste. I was expected to conform, but I never did. I went the opposite way. So even when I went into the Special Forces, I knew that what I was doing wasn't the norm. I was doing stuff that people would envy, but that a lot of people would hate to do. Some people just aren't that way inclined. And I shouldn't be smug, because after the numbness and elation associated with becoming a Special Forces soldier had worn off, I wasn't entirely satisfied either.

On completing Selection, I was so proud to make that phone call to Mum, and she was over the moon that her son was in the SBS. I got to wear the fabled blue tracksuit in camp, which gave me a lot of kudos. I felt cool as anything, walking into the mess hall in that tracksuit. Girls would nudge each other and whisper behind their hands: 'Look, SBS...' I also got to walk past the office of my old sergeant, the guy who told me how overjoyed he would be when I failed. I gave him a big smile, a little wave and a thumbs-up, and he completely ignored me. But the reality was a bit more complicated.

I had bust a gut to get into the Special Forces and it was a case of, 'Really? Is this it?' Weirdly, I liked being pushed to the absolute limit. So having only recently passed Selection, I was already missing it. There was always pressure to perform on Selection. I missed the competition, testing myself against others. Maybe that's not surprising, considering how much time I spent doing it.

After summer leave, I joined up with my troop and did lots of different courses to bring me up to speed with the rest of the team. We were sent on a combat dive course straightaway, because the SBS have a commitment to protect all British maritime assets as their primary role, which requires water-borne insertion techniques. Some people do that dive course and realise it's not for them – they can't clear their ears or they encounter other issues – and switch to the SAS. You're only diving to three metres, it's just a means of transit, but so much can still go wrong in the pitch black of the night, usually after you've gone to target and removed your breathing set.

It's dangerous work in the Special Forces and accidents happen. But that's what you sign up for. There was one exercise, which I wasn't on, that involved the lads chucking their MIBs (Military Inflatable Boats) out of the helicopter, parachuting after them, inflating the MIBs, jumping in, firing up the engines, chasing down the destroyer and inserting. They were about to get on the destroyer when the skipper realised he was getting too close to the shore and whacked it into reverse. The MIBs got pulled under and the lads got sucked into the destroyer's propellers. Luckily they missed the props but one guy was almost snapped in half on the rudder and broke both his femurs. Another time, a guy was sitting on top of a submersible insertion craft, doing what he had to do, and there was a massive swell, which crushed his head between the insertion craft and a helicopter above.

Just before I joined, a good mate of mine died doing some freefall jumping out in the States. He had a parachute malfunction, and the drill when that happens is to cut away your main to release the reserve. But his main got caught on the buckle of his dummy weapon, which should have been removed, and then went straight into his reserve. He fell 25,000 feet and ended up a pile of mush in the middle of the desert. He was a great guy who never let go of his friends from his previous career in the Marines, which some people in the service disliked him for. Later I found his grave where he died and painted his faded name back into the stone.

All the time I was training – a lot of which took place on oil rigs, practising counter-terrorism and the release of hostages – we were on call with 30 minutes notice to move. About seven or eight months after I joined my team, I was mooching around Poole one weekend when my pager went off. My first thought was, 'This must be a drill.' Then I saw the code and knew it was real. It is difficult to describe the excitement I felt, but just imagine it: one minute you're doing a bit of shopping, the next you're being asked to pull on the black gear and go into action. I guess there is something of the Superhero about it.

I rushed back to camp, where all my kit was already stowed and ready to go, and straight into an in-brief. We were told there was a ship coming into British waters loaded with drugs, and that intelligence had reason to believe they were armed and dangerous. Luckily, so were we, which is why they'd called us. It was our job to intercept the ship, take down anyone on board and hand the ship over to the authorities. But not one bit of me was scared, because this is what I'd joined for and I was ready for anything.

Our whole troop was put on a frigate out at sea, where we had to wait. That was desperately frustrating for all of us. There were 16 highly trained soldiers, raring to get on that ship and do our thing, the testosterone was pumping, the anxiety was building, and the whole time we knew that the job could be called off at any moment. Not that we were sitting around playing cards. For weeks, we ran mock-ups, planned and briefed until we could visualise exactly what might happen when – or if – the time came to execute. And because no plan survives first contact, a lot of what we did was contingency planning – or planning for any plans we'd made that might not go to plan.

Eventually, and to my relief, the call came for us to go. Seconds later, I was sitting on the boat, making its way to target under the cover of night – dressed head to toe in black, including the balaclava, and holding my assault weapon with the laser-dot sight – and it was everything I thought it would be when I was a kid; the kind of thing my careers officer would have laughed at had I suggested it.

But just as I was thinking, 'This. Is. Fucking. Amazing', the engine on my boat started spluttering. Suddenly I was thinking, 'Fuck, no! Please don't do this to me!' My world was falling apart. The other boat was fine and heading off into the distance, and we knew that if our engine didn't spring back to life, they'd have to go on without us. All that planning, all those rehearsals, possibly for nothing... and then the engine kicked in again.

In the Special Forces, we always have two plans. One is when the shit hits the fan and you just have to go in hard and hope everything goes well, the other is the plan of your choosing, when you have more time to dictate the outcome.

Usual protocol is to hit the target at dawn, so that by the time we've taken the target, we have the benefit of daylight to handover and extract. This was the case with my first job. The transit was quite a long one, but eventually I could make out the target in the gloom. It was a big, long sailing boat with masts, which had been anchored out at sea for a few weeks. There had been a massive exchange, the contraband was on board and we hoped that the enemy – or X-Rays, as we call them in the Special Forces – were tucked up in bed and fast asleep.

When I heard, 'Stand by, two minutes', I knew it was almost on, which is when the negative feelings and thoughts started flooding in: what if we board the boat and there are gunmen waiting for us? What if I get shot? I had to wrestle with that fear, pin it down and incapacitate it in order to focus on the mission, which was such a leap from anything I'd done in the 'green' Army.

Mine was the first boat to the target and I was the first man in. That's not to say I was the best or the bravest. I was pushed forward simply because I was the new boy, the least experienced and therefore the most expendable. The team leader is the guy with the most experience, the one who has the most to offer the group, but he's never going to be at the front of the pack. Command and control does not usually come from the front, because when it comes to the crunch and people could get shot, you have to protect your best asset.

The engines on MIBs aren't particularly noisy, so we were able to get straight into the hold of the ship without being detected. We headed for the sleeping quarters, kicked open the door, threw in a flash-crash grenade, which is just meant to disorientate rather than maim or kill, and started clearing our objective. All the X-Rays had been asleep, and when my target opened his eyes, he was looking at a man dressed all in black, wearing a balaclava and pointing a machine gun at his face. What a thing to wake up to.

As strange as it might sound, I felt sorry for him. He had been out on this ship for so long, done this huge deal and would have been imagining a better future. Now he had a laser dot between his eyes, I could see the fear, panic and loss and his world falling apart. I was only 24 years old and this guy had scars all over his face and looked nasty as hell. I stood there thinking, 'If this was down the pub, he'd probably give me a run for my money.' But the fact that he wasn't in a position to do so gave me such a massive feeling of power.

They were hardened criminals, had all probably done time, but we could smell the piss and the shit immediately. I don't blame them, because they had no idea who we were. We could have been members of a rival drug cartel, about to kill the lot of them. Luckily, we'd hit them by stealth and there were no rounds fired. If someone had been having a fag up on deck and spotted us coming, we'd have had to do things differently. They might have put their hands up, but they might have grabbed their weapons and started firing. You can have all the plans in the world and they might not make an ounce of difference. In the Special Forces, as in any branch of the military, you cannot choose your enemy. You just have to deal with whatever is thrown at you.

To some degree, you're being dictated to. But you can't let that happen for long; at some point you have to take control. When pressure starts being applied, you have to strip away everything else and focus on one thing, which is the threat. It's not really a case of being calm, it's about learning to deal with that level of pressure, which comes down to all the training that we do. If you're properly prepared, you'll be able to keep on top of your cortisol levels and see things in slow motion. It's like momentarily entering a parallel world, so that when it's over, you can never reimagine it. Afterwards you think, 'What happened? That didn't seem real.' You go somewhere else, like in *The Matrix*.

Ship seized, we got them down on the floor, snapped the plastic cuffs on and called in the support elements for extraction. A frigate came close, HMRC operators came aboard, we disappeared into the ether, before heading straight to a 'hot' debrief. The main concern was that no one from our side had been injured or killed. But it doesn't matter if the job went well or not, the debrief is essential.

I speak to people in the corporate world for whom debriefs are an alien concept. They're too busy discussing how awesome they are down the pub or running to their car because they don't want to get a bollocking. But debriefs are where lessons are learned, and the information gleaned from them is fed into future operations. Even the best operations contain some shit moments – the engine on my boat almost gave out, for Christ's sake! And when you're trained to the level we are in the SBS, you become extremely self-critical. What could we have done differently? Maybe I should have done this instead of that? Could I have stepped left instead of right? You see that same forensic self-analysis in elite sport, such as when a football team wins 5–1 and the manager will complain about the one goal they let in. It's about looking for imperfections in the apparently flawless.

That first mission was every bit as good as I thought it would be (apart from the spluttery engine) and it was what I wanted to be doing every day. To see all that training put into action was an amazing feeling. The communication between the team was almost telepathic, you knew everyone else had your back without anything having to be said. As I was thinking what should be happening, it was happening. There was such a flow to our movements and we fitted with each other perfectly. It was as if we were performing a ballet, with everyone exactly where he was meant to be at any given moment. It was seamless, harmonious and really rather beautiful.

What made our operations even more miraculous was that our little dance was often only one part of a far bigger picture. As we were inserting onto that ship on my first mission, there were other ships being hit and doors being knocked all over the UK, Europe and further afield. That level of coordinated planning is almost unbelievable. Our team, with all the Gucci gear, was like the star on top of a Christmas tree, but without all the infrastructure and everyone working in tandem, whether it was people pushing pens or working in the stores, we wouldn't have been able to do our job. It only takes one person lower down to make a mistake for the whole operation to come crashing down.

10

SQUARE PEG, ROUND HOLE

To do your first job with the Special Forces is an iconic moment. It's *Boy's Own* stuff and meant that I was finally part of the club. Even if I'd left the following day, I'd done a mission for the SBS.

A few months later, I had a massive weekend of partying planned in Bournemouth, just down the road from the base. I was heading to the pub on Friday afternoon when my pager went off. My first thought was, 'For fuck's sake, this can't be for real, I want to be out getting hammered.' I phoned to check if it was a drill and they said, 'No, come in straightaway.'

On my way back to camp I was thinking, 'This is bollocks, we're gonna be sitting on a fucking ship for another three or four weeks, and then the job might not even happen.' But when I walked in, everything was already moving fast. The Chinooks came in, we got our kit on and flew straight up to the relevant airbase. As soon as we got there, we were told we'd be hitting a ship that night. This was the dream job. No fucking around, no sitting about waiting. It was fast, it was slick and it was exactly how I wanted every job to be. It even occurred to me that I might still be able to get back in time for a proper drink-up.

There was a boat full of drugs doing drops all around the coast, with smugglers on board believed to be carrying weapons. This time I was part of a helicopter team and there was no time for rehearsals. We had to acquaint ourselves with our objective and target, study the plans of the ship, decide which teams would go where and how we would insert – and then go and do it.

When the time came for the helicopter team to insert, we fast-roped in the pitch black onto the target, which was even more difficult than it sounds. The sea was rough and the landing bridge was tiny. And because the ship was listing violently from side to side, the rope was only on target for a couple of seconds at a time. One inch to the left or right and it would have been fatal, but this was our bread and butter. We'd trained and trained for this type of thing, so it came naturally. That said, the fact that everyone managed to get on target was largely down to the skill of the pilot, one of whom was Prince Andrew. I used to call him our cabbie: 'Come on, Drives, step on it!' And he'd say, 'They're a bunch of blaggards – but a fine bunch of blaggards!'

As soon as we were on the ship, we made our way to our objective, which was the main hold. When we opened the door and poured in, we were greeted by piles and piles of cannabis, covering every inch of the floor and almost up to the ceiling. The smell almost took my face off. We all looked at each other and in a joyful tone I shouted, 'Fuck me!' As our sergeant came flying in, we were all laughing our heads off. When we saw him, we were almost on the floor: because he'd put his balaclava on in the dark, it had slipped round his head, so that his nose was hanging out of one of the eye holes and one of his ears was hanging out of the mouthpiece. Our sergeant started shouting at us, 'For fuck's sake, lads, let's deal with the threat first!', and we were an absolute mess.

Luckily, while we were in stitches, other teams had taken out three enemies on the bridge and we secured the remainder of the ship in a matter of minutes. There were five or six X-Rays on board but no casualties reported. Once again, they didn't even know we were there until they saw the guns in their faces.

As soon as supporting elements were brought in and on board, we extracted as quickly as possible. That involved getting into the boats, getting away from the target, Chinooks swooping in, lifting the boats out of the water and carrying us off. The gig was over in a heartbeat. I flew back down to my base, had the debrief, sorted my gear out and was ready to go partying late Saturday afternoon. My officer was at the same party and there were people smoking dope. We were looking at each other and smiling as if to say, 'If you only knew where we'd just been…'

* * *

Getting to play with all those big boys' toys was almost unbelievable but also a logical conclusion for someone who grew up playing with weapons and vehicles. I'd basically become the Action Man I owned as a kid, the one in the frogman's outfit.

But it's not as if I'd walk into a pub and tell everyone what I'd been up to in the Special Forces. I might tell people I was in the military, but that was it. Because the Troubles were still going on in Northern Ireland, the last thing I wanted to be gobbing off about was the fact I was in the SBS. But I could tell my family and friends. When you hear people saying, 'I was in the SAS, but I can't tell anyone – even my loved ones – anything about it', that often means they're a charlatan. We call them Walters, as in the fictional fantasist Walter Mitty.

Once, I went back home to Burton and was so proud of being in the SBS, I ended up telling a mate down the pub. This bloke laughed at me and said, 'You can't be in the SBS, because you're not allowed to tell anyone.' From that point on, I was more circumspect about who I told. I'd see other people talking shit, usually to women in pubs, and think, 'That bloke sounds like a fucking idiot, and that's how I'd be perceived if I started mouthing off about what I did.' Because people don't believe you anyway, you just come across like a tit. You might as well go around telling people you're a dolphin trainer or biscuit designer, which I did from time to time.

When I went out in Poole or Bournemouth, I didn't say a word about what I did for a living. In fact, I avoided mentioning the military altogether. A lot of the time I'd tell people I was down from Manchester. I loved the club scene, would lose myself in that world for whole weekends. I was bang into house and techno, had my own decks and would host parties in camp.

I didn't like the stigma attached to being in the military. In military towns, the 'green' army has a reputation for bad behaviour, getting crazy drunk and bashing up civilians. I didn't want to be associated with that world or stereotyped as that kind of person. While I was always a bit of a loose cannon, I was never one for fighting in pubs. There were others from the military who'd be out doing the same as me – who hated all the institutional bullshit and didn't feel like they really fitted in – but they were few and far between.

Most Special Forces soldiers wanted to hang out with the lads they worked with, but spending my spare time talking shop at barbecues because it might increase my chances of promotion was never an option. That world of networking, talking to people you wouldn't normally talk to and don't necessarily like, filled me with dread. I just wanted to do my work, get out of there, do my own thing and have a good time.

It's an amazing feeling to know that you're one of the few. You see people walking around acting hard and think, 'You've got no fucking idea, mate.' That gives you a sense of power and responsibility. But being in the SBS was a personal thing for me, all about the pride that I'd managed to get in.

A lot of the guys in the Special Forces detached themselves from anyone who wasn't. They wanted to spend all their time among the same kind of people, a bit like people when they become famous. But for me, it was just a job. I still had my old mates from the Marines, because I didn't think I was suddenly superior to them.

I always needed to see the purpose in everything, so I asked a lot of questions. And asking questions didn't always go down well. Asking questions shows an inquisitive mind, which some people see as a threat. The majority of the training was excellent, but there were moments that would cause me to ask why. Scenarios would be built that wouldn't make sense to me. But whenever I raised my doubts, the reply was always, 'Shut the fuck up. We're doing it just because.'

The jobs were special, and I had a lot of laughs with the lads. But there wasn't enough of that good stuff going on. It's not like I'd return from a mission and immediately be sent off to train for the next one. I'd have to wait for my pager to go off again, and that might take months. And when my pager did go off, that didn't mean the job would go through. I might be sat in a hangar for weeks before being stood down.

Unsurprisingly, that led to us taking risks. One weekend, me and another lad were driving up to Manchester – which is a fair few hours from Poole – when we got the call. An incident had gone off at Stansted Airport and we had to tell the bosses that we were halfway up the M6. Instead of getting a bollocking, we were blue-lit all the way to Essex, with a different police unit from each county picking us up on the borders and clearing the route. We were screaming through red lights, bouncing over roundabouts and laughing all the way. But as soon as we got to Stansted, we were stood down. That was incredibly frustrating, and it happened all the time. All that adrenalin, and suddenly you were being told to return to camp and shine your buttons.

I wasn't settled or satisfied, just as I hadn't been in the Royal Marines. Which makes me think being a soldier was never really my calling. I didn't want to be there, I felt I should have been somewhere else. This was the dream job, I was part of a gang that people write books and make films about. But the reality is always different to the dream. My partner Laura often says, 'I can't imagine you being in the SBS.' To which I reply, 'I can't either.'

The Special Forces was always an alien world to me, I was a square peg who had been hammered into a round hole. Being in the Special Forces was almost like a hobby. I was like a tourist, someone who popped in occasionally, before popping out again. I never gave that job the respect it deserved. Something is wrong if you're in the Special Forces and all you want to do is go clubbing. I sometimes wish I was in the SBS now, because my mindset at the age of 48 suits the job better. Youth is wasted on the young.

Recently, Foxy took me through a checklist of what people go through when they're suffering from mental illness, and one of the things he mentioned was never being settled or satisfied in your work. It was only when he told me this that I realised my mind had never been right throughout my time in the military. It didn't matter that I was, on paper, doing an exciting job, I was still unhappy. And I'd never really been happy. I never felt settled in the military. My head was so busy all the time, there was no peace of mind, because I was constantly questioning what I was doing and why I was doing it.

That's why I used to drink so much, because it would block that noise out, numb everything and cut me adrift. On the face of it, I was a fun drunk. But it wouldn't be one night, I would drink for days, until I had to stop because of work. And then I'd have to go through the torture of cold turkey, when the demon comes knocking on your door as soon as your head hits the pillow and all you can think about is having another drink to numb your thoughts.

I didn't see myself as an alcoholic, because it wasn't as if I had a bottle of whisky on my bedside cabinet. But I couldn't imagine a life without drinking. It was a crutch, especially in social situations. In the military, everyone always has a beer in their hands, so drinking helped me to integrate. Before I joined the military, I was quite judgemental about drinking. I remember my mum going to a work Christmas party, getting shitfaced and puking down my auntie's back in the car on the way home. My auntie was wearing a fur coat, so wasn't very happy. My mum ended up crawling around outside, trying to get into the house. I had some mates round, and when she crawled past the French windows I said, 'How disgusting to have a drunk as a mother', and closed the curtains. But when I went in the military, I became the opposite. That's the power of peer pressure, of wanting to feel safe in the pack.

From my mum crawling around on the floor and me being disgusted, fast forward to my brother's wedding. I was standing at the bar getting stuck into the drink when one of Justin's Royal Navy officer mates shouted: 'Naked bar!' 'Naked bar' is a Royal Marines tradition to rival wearing women's clobber. If someone from the ranks shouts 'naked bar', everyone has to take their kit off and carry on drinking as if it was the most normal thing in the world. It started in Norway, where the bars are more secluded, but soon made its way to the UK, where the bars are more crowded. You won't be surprised to hear that Marines are always being banned from pubs for doing it.

So having heard someone shout 'Naked bar!' in this posh accent, I turned around to see a load of officers stripped to the waist. Affronted, I said, 'Fucking hell, do you guys even know what naked bar is? *This* is naked bar...' With that, I stripped all my clothes off – socks, shoes, underpants, the lot – in the middle of the wedding reception, while the party was still in full swing, and carried on drinking. The rest of the night was a bit of a blur.

The following morning, Helen wasn't very impressed, although I'd fallen out with her even before I'd got naked. I went downstairs to pay the bill, still a bit jolly and acting the fool, and everyone was avoiding making eye contact with me. I asked my sister's husband why everyone looked so miserable and he replied, 'Matt, don't you fucking remember what happened last night?'

'Yeah. Naked bar. It's a Marine tradition.'

'No, not naked bar. The last time I saw you, you had your cock in your aunt's ear...'

I left the hotel pretty sharpish after that. Thankfully, my aunt saw the funny side.

Alcohol can be a positive thing. There was nothing more I wanted to do after finishing work than relax with a drink, and it certainly aided the bonding process. But alcohol can only really be a positive thing if you can control your intake, and it quickly got to the point where alcohol was controlling me.

It didn't help my overall mood that I was earning under two grand a month. When you consider what we were doing, the level of training, the commitment, the risk and the high esteem we were held in, the pay was pathetic. Some people made it work, but I never could (although that was partly down to my hectic social life), and we were being paid significantly more than regular soldiers.

If you asked people down the pub, 'What do you think a Special Forces soldier earns?', they'd be saying things like,

'Hundred grand? Quarter of a million?'. Nope. Nowhere near. And they wonder why they have a problem with retention. We do it for our country and it can be very exciting, but we've still got to pay the mortgage and the bills. I thought they were taking the piss and advantage of our patriotism. I just wanted to be rewarded properly for the job I was doing, without any catches. They'd give us bonuses, and I worked it out that they would roughly equate to a small deposit on a house. So I viewed those deposits as a devious device, because they knew that once a soldier had a mortgage, they were trapped in the military. Perhaps that's me being overly cynical, but I'm convinced there's an element of truth in it.

My colleagues weren't aware of my misgivings, because I kept them to myself. Complaining wouldn't have gone down too well with many of them, who were diehard military. Institutions such as the military want you to do as you're told, but that wasn't for me. I hated that.

I was surrounded by soldiers who were great around camp, whose boots were always shiny and who would always be on time. But you'd get them in the field and they'd perform like a bag of shit. In that respect, it was no different to working in an office, in that someone who turns up on time every day and stays later than everyone else might be terrible at the job but will still impress the bosses. As a soldier in peacetime, you get noticed more for the stuff you do in camp than in the field, but I couldn't handle the monotone existence of being a camp soldier. That's why I'd go out partying and turn up late the next day, because the partying and the drinking were substitutes for the jobs we weren't doing.

When I was partying and going wild on camp, even during the week, some of my troop sergeants would try to rein me in.

But they couldn't. Other troop sergeants could see a bit of themselves in me and tolerated my behaviour. People imagine the Special Forces to be this slick, disciplined group of people. But that's not an accurate picture. The SAS and SBS are a bunch of mavericks who can, and will, get the job done when needed. That goes back to its roots, when they were thrown together in the Second World War. They were guys who would do whatever it took. They weren't about following orders and seeking higher command – 'I've got the target in my sights, can I take the shot? Oh, he seems to have gone now' – they got things done and got the fuck out of there.

But even within that Special Forces environment, some leaders aren't able to accommodate non-conformists. Non-conformists are too often written off as misfits and therefore impossible to manage. That's how I was viewed in the SBS, because I always wanted to be different. Not better, just different. Even when we did psychometric testing, I got different results from everyone else. I was a pain in the arse. I asked too many questions. I wanted to know why, instead of just doing things. I thought asking questions was a positive trait, not a negative. I wanted to create my own path, not walk in other people's footprints.

The odd job would come up, which I would get very excited about. But afterwards I'd be back in camp again. There was always the hope that at any given moment, your pager might go off and a few hours later you might be jumping out of a helicopter. And every time I'd be thinking about leaving, one of those jobs would come up. But it wasn't enough. I wanted it to be high-octane 100 per cent of the time, not once in a blue moon. So, after about a year in the SBS, I put in my notice to leave.

* * *

I had my notice in to leave for a big chunk of my military career, which tells you everything you need to know about my ambivalence towards the job. Maybe if someone had sat me down and told me I was making a terrible mistake, like the officer who suggested I join in the first place, it might have changed my mind. But no one did, and I probably wouldn't have listened to them anyway. I was adamant that I was leaving and going outside. Then another job came up, my enthusiasm returned, and I took my notice out again. That happened three times during my six-year stay in the SBS. And because I always seemed to be on my way out, I was never considered or interested in promotion.

Looking back, I realise I wasn't only bored of peacetime soldiering, I feared the apparent predictability of my future. It sounds crazy, that I'd consider a job in the Special Forces too predictable, but I wanted to do more with my life. This was deep thinking for a soldier in his mid-twenties, but the reason people get stuck in a rut is because they don't think. And if they do think, often the conclusion they come to is, 'It's only thirty years until I retire, I might as well settle with what I've got. Stay in as long as I can and get extended service. That would be the easiest thing to do…'.

I could see the journey ahead if I stayed in the military. Circling up the ranks, doing the same thing, over and over again. I knew people who'd done that and I could see they weren't happy. Why would I want to do the same? It was another break point in my life: I could either carry on pootling along or I could veer off-road and take a more unfathomable but potentially more fulfilling route. The choice was mine.

Below: I have great memories of primary school – but secondary school wasn't for a non-conformist like me.

Above: Trouble always found me as a kid – on holiday in France, some exploding lemonade bottles cut open my legs.

Below: The Royal Marines opened their doors for me when I needed, and now as an ambassador for the Royal Marines Charity it's my turn to help the veterans and families of this prestigious unit.

Above: My pass-out parade in 1990, before deploying to 45 Commando in Scotland. Troy (left) is still my best mate.

Left: Looking mischievous before getting drunk – and naked – at my brother's wedding. But booze wouldn't always be so fun.

Right: With my brother Justin and my sister Ashley at Mum's second marriage to Simon.

Left: Justin, me and Dad at my pass-out parade. But it was Mum who put me on the straight and narrow – I owe it all to her.

Left: Close Quarters Battle training demands a lot from a soldier, testing each operator to their limit, physically and mentally.

Right: I lost about 10kg during Selection – but what amazes me now is how young I looked.

Below: Completion of Special Forces training in Poole, 1995 – the pass rate is less than 10%.

Right: In Iraq with a damaged enemy vehicle – the shoot-out on the road to Baghdad was an important break point.

Left: A close protection security job in Baghdad – I'm holding one of Saddam Hussein's Republican Guard's blinged-up AK47s.

Below: Fool's gold – from paying war lords to covering Iraqi staff wages, cash was king in Iraq and there was plenty of it.

Above: Doing business the Baghdad way – my mate Denny and I in cheap local suits and tooled-up to the max.

Right: In Thailand, we rescued 22 children from human traffickers – but a life-changing trip would eventually turn sour.

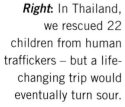

Left: After some intense visualisation, my company Break-Point was born – here I am working with my oppo Mark 'Billy' Billingham on Mission Evade.

Right: Working on Mission UK, another two-day event with Break-Point – the public love getting a taste of Special Forces Selection.

Left: In Portugal skydiving, which is my solace and escape – it's not everybody's idea of relaxation but I love the freedom it gives me.

Right: My *SAS: Who Dares Wins* buddy Jason Fox shared my dream of starting Break-Point.

Left: Celebrity *SAS: Who Dares Wins* took us back to Chile – never let it be said that celebrities aren't tough.

Right: The Directing Staff of *SAS: Who Dares Wins* – Jason, Ant Middleton, me and Billy.

Left: Series four of *SAS: Who Dares Wins* in Chile – the show is the ultimate stage for my dreams.

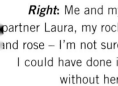

Right: Me and my partner Laura, my rock and rose – I'm not sure I could have done it without her.

Left: Building a relationship with my son Luke on a visit to Manchester – he'll be a man soon enough.

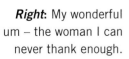

Right: My wonderful um – the woman I can never thank enough.

The most important thing in life is to help others – I formed the charity StrongMen wit recruits from *SAS: Wh Dares Wins*, Efrem Brynin and Dan Cross.

StrongMen.org.uk

11

OVER AND OUT

We spent a lot of time in the SBS training special forces from other countries. On the way to one far-off country, where we were teaching special forces soldiers jungle warfare, my team got pissed at the airport and I missed the flight. I had to be flown into Miami and spent the night there partying while the rest of the boys were building the camp. By the time I arrived in the jungle, the camp was half-built and all I had to do was assemble my camp bed. Everyone was looking at me as if to say, 'You jammy bastard.'

One of the things we taught was spy rigging, which is when you drop down the rope from the helicopter to get troops off the ground as quickly as possible. Often, the foreign guys had never been in a helicopter, so when they were lifted through the winch hole, all you could see and hear were their arms and legs squirming all over the place and their terrified screams.

There wasn't a lot to do in the jungle at night, so some of the lads would spend their downtime fishing in the river. The river was brown with mud, but they were pulling out these giant piranhas with great big teeth. During the pre-brief for the diving phase, the officer was giving us the instructions and I was looking around thinking, 'This can't be right, there are giant piranhas in that river, we've seen the fucking things! Surely they'll call it off.' Eventually, I couldn't hold back any longer, so I said, 'The lads have been pulling out giant piranhas with razor-sharp teeth all week. Last I heard, piranhas eat people, has anyone considered that?' As was always the case when you questioned their authority, they gave me short shrift.

Nevertheless, when it came to the Monday morning, I was certain the diving would be cancelled. But during the brief, an officer said, 'We've sourced these packets of shark repellent. When you're swimming along, if you feel something nibbling your legs, remove your breathing apparatus, bite the packet and shake it in the direction of the nibbles.' I couldn't believe it. I thought it was an elaborate wind-up. Alas, no, he was being deadly serious.

We had to swim in buddy pairs, with a leash between us. When we got out, my partner said, 'Why were you swimming like a weirdo, with your knees tucked up into your chest?'

'Because the first thing those giant piranhas were going to eat were my dangly legs, so I made yours the first on the menu!'

Afterwards, the officers came up with this cock and bull story about the piranhas only eating fruit. How exactly the piranhas knew the difference between a nice, juicy tangerine and one of my bollocks was anyone's guess.

Some European special forces were training with us one day, doing jungle insertions from helicopters. After we'd fast-roped in and were waiting for the command to move off, all we could hear was this horrible moaning and wailing. People were shushing and telling each other to shut the fuck up, but this voice started saying, 'I have wood', in a foreign accent. Now people were sniggering. Then someone said, 'Quick! Medic!' It transpired that this guy had hit a branch on his way to the ground and it had gone in through his arse and out through his groin on the other side, before snapping off. I'd wager that was the most painful wood he ever had. At least he got lucky with the exit wound.

We also did a lot of river skills, taking small insertion craft with very quiet engines down tributaries and creeks. One night, we dropped some lads miles away, so that they could carry out a long-range insertion. When they didn't come back in the allotted time, we had to scramble helicopters to find them. People were starting to panic, until about 12 hours later, when word came back that they'd been found. The lads had hit major torrents and rapids and were hanging on for dear life to rocks and trees. They'd lost everything – the boats, their weapons and some very expensive, sensitive gadgetry. It turned out that the second-in-command had done the recce in a helicopter about a mile up, so he hadn't seen the torrents and rapids through the canopy. Luckily, no one died, but it was a monumental fuck-up.

As well as training in the jungle, we'd also spend time in colder climes, training in Arctic warfare, and it was always big news in the local media when the British Special Forces were in town, in their big power boats with guns all over the place.

The dive package started the day after we arrived, but I was still up for going on the piss. That's just the way I was, I had to take everything to extremes. Some of the lads needed persuading, but it was Valentine's Day and I sent them over the edge by suggesting that their wives and girlfriends would probably be back home shagging other blokes anyway.

I managed to scramble a few lads together and when we walked into this club, the women were all over us. We didn't have to say anything, they were expecting us. I ended up going back to this girl's place, slept through my alarm and when I woke up it was 8:20, and the dive package had started at 8. My immediate thought wasn't, 'Fuck! I need to get there as soon as possible', it was, 'Oh well, I'm in the shit anyway, I might as well enjoy it.' So I grabbed the girl, pulled her towards me while singing

'Rule Britannia' and had a bit more fun. It certainly beat being submerged in a freezing fjord.

My snooze was broken by a loud banging on the door. I thought it had to be one of her friends, but when she came back she told me it was my soldier mates. I was lying there thinking, 'How the fuck do they know I'm in this girl's apartment?' Because I'd gone missing, my bosses had contacted the police, who had visited the club owner. He'd gone through the CCTV and seen which girl I'd left with, so knew exactly where to find me. When I got back to base, I got the mother of all bollock-ings. But I was always doing shit like that. It was almost like I was trying to get thrown out, but it didn't work. They said they weren't going to tell HQ, and I was allowed to carry on with the dive package.

After three days' diving, we returned to HQ. We were having dinner, with the hierarchy sat at the top table, all chatting away, when the local liaison officer walked in with a newspaper under his arm. He made a beeline for the top table and in a very loud voice said, 'I see you have been in the newspaper again?' The commanding officer replied, 'Really? What for?' The liaison officer opened the newspaper very theatrically and started reading, as loud as he could, 'Last night, one of the British Special Forces Commandos went missing. Helicopters were scrambled but they failed to locate the whereabouts of him. They feared for his life and thought he may have been killed, however he was later found in bed with a local hairdresser...'

My head fell on the table. All the talk about the story not getting back to HQ and it had made the bloody newspaper. Everyone was in hysterics, even the top brass saw the funny side.

I did my job well, so managed to get away with things. But it's fair to say that when I wasn't doing my job, I was a loose cannon.

I burnt the candle at both ends, it was all or nothing. My life was a big ball of mayhem, but for a while I thrived off it.

* * *

My best mate at the time was a guy called Mick. Me and Mick loved the social aspect of the Special Forces, were thick as thieves and always getting into mischief. One night back in the jungle, I was sitting around with Mick in camp and I noticed that the bank notes had pictures of gold bullion and diamonds on them. Our minds started racing and we were soon discussing getting hold of some diamonds and working out how to get them home.

On our last night, the British Embassy threw a party, as a thank-you for training the local forces. As luck would have it, we were introduced to a diamond dealer. We told him we wanted to come back and do a deal, after we'd completed Arctic warfare training. So when the three months of snow and ice were up, we returned to the UK, got a load of money together and flew back to the jungle.

Not long after we arrived, we were walking down this mud road, surrounded by cattle, when we saw a Chinese guy being mugged and macheted. It was like one of those lawless towns you see in old Wild West films, except more dangerous. Undeterred, we met our contact and bought £20,000-worth of cut diamonds, before jumping straight on a flight to a neighbouring country.

We were cock-a-hoop, sitting in our hotel room, surrounded by empty beers and telling each other, 'We're fucking diamond dealers! This is going to change our lives! I'm leaving the SBS as soon as we get home!'

After a day on the piss, Mick said, 'We need to mark this moment.'

'Shall we get matching tattoos? Or bracelets?'

'Fuck that. Let's get gold teeth, like gangsters.'

We ended up in the dentist, getting perfectly good teeth filed down. Someone was sent out with some money to buy the gold, the dentist melted it down into caps and popped them in our mouths. For the next few days, we were sat in the bar flashing these gold gnashers to everyone, chuffed as anything. Mine lasted for years and I've still got it in a box somewhere.

On the day of the flight home, we split the bags of diamonds between us, stuffed them in condoms and swallowed them. But when we got to the airport, we looked up at the destinations board to see that our flight was delayed for 24 hours. So we had to go back to our rooms, shit them out, polish them off and go through the same process 24 hours later. When we finally arrived at Gatwick, we made it through customs and Mick went straight to the toilet and shit his diamonds out again. My dad had come to pick us up and when we got to his car he said, 'I know you've been up to no good but I don't want to know anything about it.' Me and my dad weren't close, but he still knew me too well.

I went back to my dad's place in Basingstoke and Mick went back up to Manchester. Then, for the next 24 hours, Mick was on the phone to me every minute, paranoid that I'd already shit my share of the diamonds out and hadn't told him. And all the time, I was thinking, 'Maybe they've disappeared somewhere inside my body? Maybe they'll appear in my bloodstream? Or they're stuck in my bladder and I'll have to piss them out instead?'

Finally, and to my enormous relief, I needed a shit. Having done the deed, I dropped to my knees over the toilet bowl and began sifting through my own excrement with my hands. But after a couple of minutes, I had to conclude that the diamonds weren't in there. I collapsed on the toilet floor, my gold tooth throbbing and my hands covered in my own shit, and fell asleep thinking, 'Oh, the glamour of being a diamond dealer…'

Luckily, the next time I went to the toilet, the diamonds dropped out. Through an officer at the camp in Poole, we ended up taking them to Asprey, one of the most exclusive jewellers in London, to get them valued. They weren't good enough for Asprey to use, but some of the things we saw in that place made the mind boggle. We were taken into a lift and led into this room that contained shopping bags full of bank notes and just about every item you could think of encrusted in diamonds. There were diamond-encrusted guns, diamond-encrusted bikes, there was even a diamond-encrusted dildo. At least that's what I think it was.

We ended up selling some of the diamonds to our mates for their girlfriends' engagement rings. The wife of one of my best pals Tim was out for lunch with her girlfriends recently when the subject of engagement rings came up. They were going around the table, each giving the story behind their ring – 'Mine's from Tiffany', 'Mine's from Harrods', 'Mine was handed down from Charlie's grandma' – until the conversation reached Sara. 'Well,' she said, 'the diamond on my engagement ring came out of Tim's mate's arse...'

* * *

Eventually, I moved to a squadron that specialised in more conventional soldiering. Our primary commitment was as a mountain troop, specialising in mountain warfare. Our secondary role was as VIP security. One day, we were climbing in the South-West when the team commander's pager went off. In no time at all, we were filling up the vehicles and heading back to Poole. In Poole, we loaded up our kit, got straight on the motorway and headed to the airport. When we got to the airport, we drove straight across the runway in these blacked-out wagons before loading our weapons onto this commercial British Airways plane. God knows what the air hostesses were thinking.

The plane was bound for Asia, specifically a country that had descended into economic chaos and civil unrest. Our job was to secure and protect all British Embassy staff, make evacuation plans and await extraction, but before that there was a good time to be had. We were ushered into first class, then the air hostesses started popping champagne. That was one hell of a party. Once at our destination, we started working on the evacuation plans, but it never came to that, so we got stood down and sent back home. The anti-climaxes were piling up, and it was beginning to really grind me down.

There is a lot of talk about post-traumatic stress disorder in relation to the military, and rightly so. But a lot of the stress in the Special Forces isn't caused by traumatic events, it's caused by the toing and froing of emotions. My emotions were all over the place, because we would go from sheer boredom to eye-popping excitement in the click of a finger. And on so many occasions, the adrenalin would froth and the blood boil to no end. No wonder I spent so much time in nightclubs: at least I knew I'd get a buzz in there.

It was around this time, in 1998, that I decided I wanted to fulfil my childhood dream of learning to pilot a submersible insertion craft. So I applied to do a four-month course in America, working with the Navy SEALs. Shortly after arriving, I bleached my hair white and went and bought a surfboard. Suddenly, I wasn't there to learn how to pilot a submarine, I was there to have a great time in the sun. Recently, a Navy SEAL mate sent me a picture of me on the beach. You never would have suspected I was Special Forces, I looked like a hippy or a beach bum. That was me saying, 'I am my own man, you can't tell me what to do, I'll do what I want,' which was the same as my departure from school.

Looking back, I think I actually wanted to piss people off. It was about achieving little victories, getting little jabs in. What did it matter what my hair looked like? I could do the job well – shoot in a straight line and get to target – and that's all I cared about. Fuck all the stupid rules.

With the benefit of hindsight, this anger and frustration at being straitjacketed was further proof that I was in the wrong job. I wasn't able to find any flow or purpose because I was living the life of a person I thought I was supposed to be. It's why I was a good, effective soldier, but never a typical soldier. Or a contented one. My true self was inside somewhere, but I never discovered who that was until I left the military.

I did do some work in America. Best of all, I got to prove that careers officer wrong by learning to pilot that submersible insertion craft, just as I told her I would do. But when I returned to the UK, it all went wrong again. I thought I was going to a squadron in which I would have utilised my new skills. But I didn't get the placement. I couldn't believe it. They'd spent all that money on me to train in the States and they were sending me back to my old squadron. So I thought, 'Fuck this, I'm leaving.' They couldn't believe it either. But I'd made my mind up. What was the point in staying, if they weren't going to allow me to use my skills?

So, once again, I put my notice in. I'd done it several times before, but this time I meant it. I was comfortable in the military, but something was missing, and always had been. That time had finally come to veer off-road and take that more unfathomable but potentially more fulfilling route.

I served my year's notice and although I didn't get any seniority, I was made a team leader, which was unheard of for someone on their way out. But I spent most of my time getting ready to go outside, and most of my last six months at home. Before I left, I had to go and see the commanding officer of the SBS. When I walked into his office, the CO was sat behind his desk and my sergeant major and troop officer were also there. The CO started reading out my testimonial and I couldn't believe what I was hearing. It was fucking amazing! All the way through my career, I'd been a pain in the arse on camp, and now I was being told what a wonderful soldier I'd been and all the great things I'd achieved. One part of me had always known I was a good soldier, but another part of me was convinced my superiors thought otherwise, because of my refusal to conform. I was looking at my sergeant major and troop officer and thinking, 'Has he got the right bloke?'

When the CO finished, he said, in his classic officer's accent, 'There seems to be some kind of error here that will need to be corrected.'

And I replied, 'What, my fucking name?'

My sergeant major and troop officer erupted in laughter. My CO had no idea what they were laughing at. Like I say, not everybody got me in the SBS.

12

PEACE IN WAR

That was that. I was ex-military. A former soldier. A civilian. But there were no regrets. I'd been gagging to get out. There was a big blank canvas out there that I needed to make my mark on. I just didn't know what that mark was going to look like.

I'd done no planning whatsoever. Soldiers leave the military with the attitude, 'Yoo-hoo! It's me! Come and get me!' Meanwhile, people are thinking, 'Who the fuck is this bloke?' It's not an uncommon phenomenon with any significant career change. But I think it's particularly prevalent in the military. Before long, these soldiers can sink into a depression and start thinking, 'What the hell have I done? Why does no one want me? Am I worthless? Am I good for nothing if I'm not a soldier?'

I did know I wanted to carve a new path, be a salesman, learn negotiation and start my own business. I felt that the only way I'd be satisfied was if I was my own boss. But it didn't work out like that. It's common for soldiers to leave the Special Forces and go straight on 'the circuit', which mainly consists of surveillance work, security for companies operating in warzones, as well as for high-profile VIPs and showbiz people. And a lot of people left the Special Forces about the same time as I did, because they were frustrated at the lack of action. They didn't want to be marking time, were afraid of a predictable future and wanted more out of life. There was more going on – and a lot more money to be made – outside of the military.

I'd never planned to go on the circuit full-time, but the jobs paid incredibly well, and usually in cash. So I started doing bits and bobs to keep my head above water. I did some personal training, some security work in London, some work for HMRC. It was all word of mouth, not the kind of work you got offered at Job Club – 'Mr Ollerton, we've got a job stacking shelves in Lidl or a job doing security for Madonna...' And before I knew it, I couldn't get off the circuit. I was on the list. I was a hamster in a wheel, conforming to type.

Soon, my relationship with Helen started to deteriorate. The first thing she said to me when I walked through the door, having just returned from SBS camp, was: 'You're not going anywhere.' That was like a red rag to a bull. I felt like turning around and walking straight out. I had thought that leaving the military would strengthen our bond, but it went the other way. I'd been with her since 1991 and this was nine years later. But during that time, I'd only seen her on weekends here and there. We'd never lived with each other consistently. Every time I came home on leave, we'd have some quality time together and we knew there would be an end to it. That kept the relationship fresh, and the first few years were great. But when that dynamic changed, things started spiralling out of control.

My drinking got worse. Being a civilian allowed me more flexibility, and I spent a lot of my spare time on the booze. I was using it to drown out the monotonous white noise of everyday civilian life. The discipline and routine of the military had gone and there was no reason not to booze when the chance arose. And the chance arose a lot. Helen was drinking a lot, too, and the arguments became more regular and more vicious.

Of course my time in the military was hazardous, but the Special Forces contained me, because it was a semi-controlled environment. As I've already outlined, I got into a fair few scrapes while I was serving. But before and after serving were chaotic times, which proves that the military doesn't always manage to reform people. I had no focus or direction, didn't know what I'd be doing from one week to the next. That put pressure on me and it put pressure on Helen. Some women crave the security of a partner with a solid nine-to-five job and a regular wage. I can understand that. But I was never going to be that man. In fact, I already knew that it was probably best that we shouldn't be together at all.

Luke was born in June 2001 and it was a blessing to have such a beautiful little boy. We'd decided not to find out the sex of the baby, so when he came out, I burst into tears. I had a little companion to do stuff with, whether it be yomping through the countryside or climbing up mountains. I thought I would bring him up to be a little version of me, although I'm not sure that would have been a good thing at the time.

For a short while, being a dad was glorious. But it didn't hide the marital problems. We were still arguing all the time, it's just that now we were doing it in front of our baby. Luke was like a Band-Aid for our relationship, but kids should never be used in that way. Getting married and having a child didn't bring us closer together, all it did was make it harder to escape from an obviously dysfunctional relationship. So many couples make the same mistake, thinking that bringing another human into this earth makes more sense than splitting up. The truth is that some people are just not meant to be with each other.

Five months after Luke was born, we got married, and the wedding provided plenty more clues that all was not right with the relationship. When I did my speech, I got to the end and realised

I hadn't even mentioned Helen. I spent most of the time trying to make my best man Tim laugh. She didn't say anything, but she clearly wasn't happy. Let's just say it wasn't your classic, harmonious wedding day. The honeymoon wasn't a fairy tale either.

Even before I married Helen, I felt that the only way I was going to get away from her was through a divorce. I felt I had to carry on down that road until I reached a dead end, and only then would I be able to resolve the situation. So many people end up trapped in similar situations until it reaches the stage when the hassle of staying in ceases to trump the hassle of getting out. We had a house together, our lives were intertwined on so many different levels, and I don't think I could have coped with the confrontation and disruption. I had nowhere to go, no settled job. I couldn't handle the thought of my life getting worse. I was existing in an uncomfortable comfort zone. Just as I'd intended to leave the military on several occasions, but was unable to because the world beyond it seemed so unknowable, I was unable to bite the bullet and leave Helen. Throughout that relationship, break points were coming and going without me even noticing them.

I did manage to escape the circuit for a while. I had a friend called Karl who was one of those blokes who always had a nice suit and car and a big wad of cash in his hand. He had so much energy, was a great salesman and was who I wanted to be.

One day, Karl got in touch and said in his deep, gravelly northern accent, 'Matt, do you want a job?'

'Doing what?'

'Selling orange juice machines.'

'How much?'

'You could earn a grand a week.'

Compared to what I'd been earning in the SBS, this was mega-money.

Karl sold franchises to sell these Orange Olé juicing machines, as they were called. You bought a franchise, were given a postcode, got given ten machines, gave them to restaurants and shared the juice profits 50-50. And for every machine I managed to offload, I got 100 quid.

I was given an area in Cornwall, which was perfect: my family was down there, so it would almost be like a working holiday. On my hit list was a cafe on Lusty Glaze Beach, this beautiful secluded cove near Newquay. There was no access by road, so I had to carry this machine down a load of steep steps. As I descended, I couldn't help having a little chuckle to myself: here I was with an orange-juicing machine on my back, when only a few years earlier I would have been doing something similar with a pack on my back, on the Brecon Beacons. Oh how times had changed...

I walked into this cafe and said to the owner, 'Have you got time for a demo?' The owner was a bit busy, but reluctantly said yes. So I plonked the machine on the bar, got some oranges out and started telling the owner how incredibly easy it was to use. 'In fact,' I said, 'it's so easy, I should ask one of your customers to do the demo.' At that precise moment, this surfer dude walked through the door, wearing board shorts and nothing else. So I said to him, 'If you demonstrate this orange machine for the boss, I will give you a free juice.' So this dude put the oranges in the top, put the lid back on and I said to him, 'See that button there? Just press that.' I had this cocky grin on my face, because I thought I had this deal in the bag and another 100 quid in my back pocket. The dude pressed the button and his face froze into a rather intense glare, while his hair stood on end and started smoking: the fucking machine had electrocuted him. The owner was standing there looking much the same as this poor surf dude. As was I, at least for a couple of seconds. When I snapped out of it, I grabbed the machine, chucked it on my back and legged it back up the steps as fast as my legs would carry me. It was the height of summer, about 32°C, and I was sweating like a lunatic.

When I reported the incident to head office, they told me they'd been getting calls all week. There were orange machines going wrong all over the country. One person told me that they were safe to operate as long as you were wearing shoes, which explained why the surfer dude came a cropper. Other machines were squirting juice all over people's faces and clothes, machines were being chucked on skips and people had sacks of oranges going mouldy in their garage. I'd basically walked into an episode of *Only Fools and Horses*. My mates still tease me about it now. They'll see me and start shouting, 'Olé! Olé!'

But that job selling faulty orange machines did get me onto the sales ladder, and the next thing I knew I was a regional sales manager, selling cash machines. I'd suspected I might become an RSM one day, except a regimental sergeant major in the military.

I took the job to keep Helen happy, although I can't deny that sales had always appealed to me, mainly because I thought I might be quite good at it. I was resilient and determined and all those other things the military had taught me.

I employed a load of ex-military mates to fit the machines and it actually ran quite smoothly. But I was bored shitless. Of course I was. Even being in the SBS bored me at times. Because I was now in the civilian world, I thought I had to do what civilian people did, which was dull, uninspiring jobs. I thought there must be something wrong with me. I thought my failing relationship and lack of work satisfaction was all my fault. I'd fallen into the trap of trying to keep other people happy, while not considering my own happiness.

There is a certain peace in war. There is a simplicity. It's black and white. Someone wants to kill you, and you're going to kill them if necessary. That's why soldiers feel at home in warzones and why so many of them struggle when they come home. When you're in a warzone, you're a small part of a big picture. And the mundane trivialities of civilian life aren't even in the frame.

Strange as it might sound, life in a warzone can be so much easier than life outside the military. Soldiers come home and they've got wives moaning because the neighbour has parked across the drive; or they've bought the wrong kind of cheese; or the washing machine has broken; or the flush has gone on the toilet. They're bickering with their partners about petty things. To a soldier who isn't used to dealing with such trifles, that can be extremely stressful. In fact, it can feel like mayhem, and far less normal than a warzone.

When I mentioned the concept of peace in war on *SAS: Who Dares Wins*, I got some incredible feedback. There were so many former soldiers who could relate to what I was saying. These weren't just people who had PTSD, these were people who simply found civilian life so much more challenging than being in a warzone. Even people who have lost limbs crave to go back. A mate of mine got shot in the head by an Iraqi sniper and wanted to return. It's not necessarily the danger that they miss, it's that sense of brotherhood. Being around the lads is something you take for granted, because it's such a natural, relaxed environment to be in. And then you leave. Suddenly you're having to deal with bills and painting fences and tiling bathrooms and an awful lot of white noise. Perhaps it doesn't reflect very well on civilian life, but one of the principle reasons soldiers want to return to warzones is to feel safe again.

The rows with Helen became horrendous. She was working at a Porsche dealership as a PA, and when she went on maternity leave, she put all her stuff in a white cardboard box, brought it home and plonked it in the middle of the lounge. I went on a massive bender that night and returned at about two the following morning, without my key. Helen wouldn't let me in, but I managed to break in through a window. I fell onto a couch in the lounge and the next thing I knew, Helen was standing over me, screaming and shouting. I thought the world had ended. Helen then picked up the white box and the bottom fell out, scattering her office things all over the floor. Apparently, I'd used it as a substitute toilet.

It's not as if I made a habit of coming in drunk and urinating on Helen's prized possessions, but it was undoubtedly a toxic environment for a baby to be around. Luke was no age, but kids are sponges and I knew the constant drinking and rowing must have been affecting him. Then, one fateful day, my old mate Mick called to tell me he could get me a job in Iraq in a heartbeat. As soon as he said that, my mind opened up to new possibilities.

This was early 2003, when Iraq was on the verge of descending into chaos. But I needed to be back in the fold, doing something on a bigger scale, something with a greater purpose than selling cash machines. The opportunity of being in a warzone and at the sharp end of something big and important was very appealing. And the money was phenomenal. The whole time I'd been in the military, I'd been in financial straits, struggling to make ends meet. And now I was being offered £13,000 a month, tax free.

I even thought that going away again might save our relationship. However, in moments of clarity, I realised that I just wanted to get away from Helen. Society says that you must try to save a marriage, but I didn't want to. The bottom line was, I just wanted to make myself right and feel alive again.

I drove straight down to London, had a meeting with a company rebuilding the infrastructure in Iraq and they offered me the gig. The following day, Mick put me in touch with another company and I decided to work for them instead. It was raining jobs on the circuit. When I told Helen, she wasn't happy. She gave me an ultimatum: 'It's either me and Luke or Iraq.'

I was deploying to Iraq in two days' time and I had made my choice. In my head, I was already on the streets of Baghdad with a weapon concealed under my jacket. Staying with Helen would have meant more mayhem, for me, her and Luke. I thought that living in a warzone was a far less complicated option. Marriage guidance counsellors are all well and good, but sometimes you can overthink things. We didn't like each other, simple as that. Being in that relationship wasn't doing my mental welfare any good. I'd had enough and I wanted out. So I said, 'I'm going to Iraq, and that's the end of it.' Her giving me that ultimatum was the final nail in the coffin, my justification to leave. And it was the best decision for all three of us. Life might be harder in the short term, but it would get better.

13

THE ROAD TO BAGHDAD

My first job in Iraq was working as security for American network ABC News. Flying into Jordan, I wasn't worried about what I might have got myself into, I was overwhelmed with excitement at being back in the mix again.

When I reached the Jordan–Iraq border, an ex-SAS guy I knew called Ben was there to pick me up. He explained that he had some weapons buried in a cache across the border, and that as soon as we got into Iraq, we'd collect them. I was rubbing my hands together, thinking, 'I cannot wait to get back on the tools!'

Shortly after crossing into Iraq, we came to a halt and Ben shot off to pick up the weapons. When he returned, he passed me this tiny little Tokarev pistol. It was so small, I could hardly get my finger in the trigger guard. It looked like the kind of thing a female Bond villain would keep hidden in her garter, except it didn't have a mother-of-pearl handle, it had a rusty metal one.

I said to Ben, 'Are you taking the piss?'

'Don't worry about it, mate, there's not much threat about at the moment...'

I got back in the vehicle, looked at this gun and thought, 'This is pathetic...' My dreams were shattered. I was supposed to be rear protection on the transit, but I would have been better off with a sack full of rocks.

As soon as we got to Baghdad, we started our security detail for ABC. This usually involved ferrying them around the city, mostly in ones and twos. It was only a few months after the country had been invaded and Saddam Hussein's statue had been toppled in Firdos Square, so it was quite tense in Baghdad at the time. One day, a massive explosion went off near our compound. We jumped straight in our vehicles and soon came upon a building that had been reduced to a smouldering pile of rubble. The building had been the Canal Hotel, which the United Nations used as its headquarters in Iraq. We later learned that a 500-pound bomb had been delivered in a cement truck.

We were the first people on the scene and found a handful of people trapped under the rubble, one of whom turned out to be a Brazilian diplomat called Sergio Vieira de Mello. We tried to dig him out, but he died at the scene. At least 22 people died in that explosion, including a British citizen.

Because we arrived before the US military, we were taken into the inner cordon, where I started taking photos of the devastation. I didn't think anything more of it until later that night when one of the ABC journalists came to see me and asked to see my pictures. I did a deal with Associated Press and the pictures were in newspapers and on websites all over the world.

I should have got a lot more than the $2,000 Associated Press paid me, but it was enough to buy myself a laptop on the black market. When I got the laptop back to my hotel room, I asked ABC's opps people to drop an internet cable down to our room. Me and my old mate Mick were the only people on the security team with a connection and we spent a lot of time messing about on chat rooms, surfing the net and shopping. But a few days after our internet was installed, it went down, as did everyone's at ABC towers in Baghdad.

Soon we got word that all the servers had gone down at Disney, who were ABC's parent company, in America. Everything had crashed, nothing was working. Then an ABC journalist in Baghdad received a phone call from Disney HQ: 'Have you got somebody working for you called Ollie? Yes? Does he have a laptop?' The laptop I'd bought off the black market had a virus on it, and that virus had taken out the whole of Disney's network. I'd killed Mickey Mouse.

There was a tentative hope that the war was already over and the various news organisations were reassessing their need for security. We had a detail of about six guys, and we cost a couple of grand a day per person. And because security was so expensive, any opportunity a news organisation had to get rid of some people and save a bit of money, they took it.

I was made up to team leader, and my first operation was to pick up the new ABC bureau chief from Jordan and drive him back to Baghdad, which was something like a 28-hour round trip (there were no flights coming into Iraq, because of the threat of surface-to-air missiles). But it wasn't just the bureau chief I had to bring back, it was him and 11 others. And I was only allowed to take one colleague with me. And we only had access to soft-skinned civilian vehicles. In the military, it would be the other way round, 12 security personnel for two civilians. And we'd have armoured vehicles. But we were trying to keep the ABC people happy and make sure we kept getting paid, so we did it. It was a decision made against our better judgement, but what could possibly go wrong?

We knew the bureau chief was coming to assess the need for security, so on the drive to Jordan I kept thinking, 'Fucking hell, I left everything for this – my home, my wife, my child – and if this bloke decides we're not needed, it could all end tomorrow.' I was trying to get some balance back into my life, do something that made me feel alive, and this job seemed like it might be it. So I kept on telling myself, over and over again, 'This cannot possibly end.'

Every time I'd desperately wanted something to happen, I'd devoted a lot of time to visualising it. I hadn't wasted time worrying too much about the journey but stayed focused on the destination. I'd stoked the passion, lived the ultimate moment, imagined what achieving that goal would look and feel like. I did the same before joining the Royal Marines and the same before joining the SBS. By the time I got in, I'd already been there a thousand times. So when we got to the InterContinental Hotel in Amman, I was sitting at the bar with my number two, Dave, when I turned to him and said, 'Look, mate, this contract cannot end. So this is what's going to happen for them to have to extend it: we're going to leave here, pick the 12 of them up and drive them over the border. Then, somewhere between Fallujah and Ramadi, we're going to get attacked. We're going to have a gunfight, we're going to get the ABC people out of it, and when we get to Baghdad, there's going to be a heroes' welcome. And once the champagne's been popped, the bureau chief is going to sign a new contract on the spot.'

I told Dave this story in the minutest detail, made him live it with me. He thought I was joking, but I wasn't. I might have told the story in a light-hearted manner, but I was deadly serious. As strange as it might sound, I was living a moment that I desperately wanted to happen. I didn't actually think we were going to get shot at, but I did talk about it as a possibility. And when I was describing it, I could smell the cordite from the bullets. Then, having arrived at the final destination, I could taste the champagne and feel the bubbles tickling my nose. I could feel the coldness of the glass in my hand and the firmness of the bureau chief's handshake. And I could see the look of gratitude on his face.

After telling Dave my story, we got chatting to two girls who worked for British Airways. I ended up with the pilot, Dave ended up with the flight attendant, we all ended up in their rooms, and what happened, happened. That story is relevant, in case you're wondering, but you'll have to find out why later.

At 3am the following morning, we met the bureau chief and his entourage and set off in our convoy of four vehicles – four in each vehicle in front of us and me and Dave bringing up the rear. Customs on the border was a horrible experience as usual, made even worse by the amount of gear the ABC guys had with them. They were all wearing Rolex watches, they had piles of camera equipment, cases of money, and there were a lot of eyes on us. Eventually we made it through, pulled over, put our body armour on and headed for Baghdad, which was still about ten hours away...

There was not much to see on the road from Amman to Baghdad. There was sun, of course, searing a mighty hole through acre after acre of blue. Camels and goats, foraging for unseen greenery. The odd bomb crater and chewed-up vehicle, including a bright red Ferrari, which would have made more sense on the moon. And mile after mile of highway, hugged by a watery haze and cutting a swathe through the flat and featureless desert landscape. And suddenly there I was, staring into the eyes of a young boy, his AK47 pointed at my face. It was the chimpanzee attack all over again: either I lay down and accepted my fate, or I went to a less comfortable place in the hope of improving my – our – situation.

The MP5 kurz is a short weapon, but you should use it two-handed. It's difficult to describe the complexity of using a weapon like that in a close-quarter battle scenario, while trying to keep control of a vehicle travelling at 130kph. There is absolutely no margin for error, and you could end up shooting your own arm off. But I had no choice at that moment but to pull a gangster move. I popped the weapon off my lap, rested it on my arm and the boy's eyes almost popped out of his head. I shouted, 'Open fire!', before Dave and I squeezed off two sharp bursts, which shattered the closed windows on our vehicle. The enemy's car veered into the central reservation to their left, while I slammed my foot down and put as much distance as I could between our vehicle and the enemy's as quickly as possible.

It was all over in a couple of seconds. Dave and I squeezed our triggers and that was it. I don't know how many bullets hit the car, or if anyone inside was hit. There weren't Hollywood blood splatters or screams, and the vehicle didn't go up in flames and billow pink smoke. But I could see black plumes pouring from the bonnet and knew they weren't coming after us. The back-up vehicle had also slowed down, which was an added bonus.

When I looked ahead, I could see the ABC bureau chief with his hands and face pressed up against the window, his eyes like saucers. The smell of cordite singed my nostrils and my ears were filled with a piercing ringing.

As soon as it was likely that the enemy vehicles weren't coming after us, I got straight on the radio to Baghdad and told them what had happened – 'No casualties on our side, I believe there may be casualties on their side' – and headed home. Dave and I didn't say much for a few hours. We were still on high alert. It was only when we entered the relative safety of Baghdad that Dave said to me, 'Fuck me. Didn't you say that was going to happen?'

When the compound gates opened, there was a welcoming party to greet us, exactly as I'd imagined. When I got out of the vehicle, I thought I'd dropped some coins on the floor. It was the first noise I'd been able to make out since the gunfight, other than the terrible ringing. When I looked down, there were empty shell cases and shards of glass sprinkled around my feet.

Someone handed me a flute of champagne and I felt the coldness of the glass in my hand and the bubbles tickling my nose. And then the bureau chief appeared with a contract in his hand, gave me a firm handshake, and we signed on the spot. Dave must have thought I was a witch. Obviously, the news crew were over the moon, but it was a highly sensitive incident. Whenever you take that kind of action, it gets scrutinised in forensic detail. You have to be 100 per cent justified. The force needs to be appropriate, there can be no overkill. So there were no immediate pats on the back. I'm sure if we'd been engaging bandits on a regular basis, a lot of questions would have been asked. But we were confident we'd taken the correct action in exceptional circumstances, and we had three cars full of witnesses. And when the email came in from ABC bosses, we were vindicated. It read: 'We greatly appreciate your quick thinking and positive action. On behalf of all at ABC News, we'd like to say thank you and well done.'

When I was back in Special Forces, I had so many support elements. I could call in naval gunfire or an airstrike. I had so much armour. I had someone to my right, someone to my left and someone above and below. I just felt invincible. But I can't say I was angry at having ended up in such a dangerous situation. Yes, we were totally outgunned. Just from that one car that was onto us, we were outnumbered two to one. We were supposed to be the experts. But I just thought, 'This is just the way they do things in this world.' You can't do those jobs expecting military processes and protocols. They didn't have the money or the manpower. And the bottom line was, we just couldn't have turned that job down. If we had, they just would have employed another security company. The smirks on my colleagues' faces told me everything I needed to know.

Far from being upset or spooked, I was elated. All soldiers enjoy a contact. I'd have felt guilty if people on our side had been injured or killed, but it was a successful mission, the perfect scenario, a dream come true. Literally. When I went to bed that night and pulled the covers up to my chest, I did wonder about that kid and whether I'd killed him. He wasn't a soldier, he was just an opportunist and a misfit. But you can't feel guilty for long, not when the alternative was getting blasted in the face.

It was another break point in my life that made perfect sense. It was a defining and spiritual moment, and an extremely powerful one. Being attacked by that chimpanzee is still the most terrifying thing that has happened to me. But it was the break point on the road to Baghdad that had the greatest influence on me. That gunfight in Fallujah was the universe saying, 'Show this idiot that this visualisation stuff works.' Will it hard enough, see it in enough detail, invest enough emotion in it, and it will happen. I had suspected it did, but what happened on the road to Baghdad was like being knocked on the head – BOOM! I wouldn't say it changed my life on the spot – it was many years before I fully understood the implications – but it was the first step down a different path. Everything I've done since then has been a reflection of that moment, especially in recent years. Whether it was my business or the television programme, it all happened because of visualisation. It might even be the case that the first time visualisation worked in my life was when I hit the Mitchell sister with my bike, because I couldn't stop thinking about all the horrible things I wanted to do to her. So anyone who says visualisation doesn't work is missing out.

I truly believe that we all have an amazing gift, it's just that most of us don't realise we have it or are using it in a negative fashion. It sounds like hocus-pocus and it's difficult for some people to believe in, because the rewards are usually intangible in the short term. But our lives reflect our thought patterns and are the products of our imaginations. If you visualise what you want, you will make decisions and take actions that bring you closer to that goal, even if some of those decisions and actions will be a result of subconscious thinking. If you're a negative person, you will get negative outcomes. If you're a positive person, you will get positive outcomes. It's a choice we make.

A few days after the attack, a big group of us flew back to the UK, on British Airways. We were herded into cattle class at the back of the plane, but shortly after taking off one of the flight attendants opened the curtain and said, 'Is one of you Mr Ollerton?' I made myself known, took down my gear from the overhead locker and smiled at the chuntering of my colleagues. It would seem that the pilot I'd met in the InterContinental hotel had arranged an upgrade. Either Dave's girl didn't have as much clout or she wasn't as impressed. The flight attendant led me up to first class and put me in seat 1A. While the other lads were sitting with their knees up to their chins, I was reclining with a bottle of champagne. I couldn't help peering back down the aisle, raising my glass and giving my colleagues the biggest grin imaginable. And when I woke up from a nap, I found another bottle of champagne sitting next to me. I've had worse flights.

I got attacked by a chimp and met Bridget Bardot, I got attacked in Iraq and met a very accommodating pilot. However weird and messed-up the situation I find myself in, I always manage to find a gem in there somewhere. My life has always been like that. I'd find a silver lining in a mushroom cloud. But that's what happens when you have a relentlessly positive outlook.

14

TEMPTING DEATH

Shortly after that incident, I left ABC and went to work for an oil company as an independent consultant. My role was to look after two directors, ferrying them in and out of Baghdad. It was a good job and I was soon negotiating a permanent contract. Facilitating the logistics meant dealing with the boss's personal assistant, an Australian girl called Nat who worked in London. We immediately hit it off and before long were flirting with each other over the phone and via email. When I was back in London for the company's Christmas party, we arranged to meet. And from that point on, we were virtually inseparable.

It was clear that my marriage to Helen was unsalvageable, so pretty much as soon as I met Nat, I phoned and told her I wouldn't be coming home again. Nat and I found a swanky flat in Chiswick and for the first time in as long as I could remember, life was almost perfect. I didn't know life could be that good; every second I was with Nat I was like a kid at Christmas.

I never signed a contract with Nat's company, because the job would have required me spending most of my time in Baghdad and I much preferred the idea of doing six months on, six months off. But around the same time, Mick and another mate called Andy who I'd served with in the SBS set up a security company almost overnight – there was a lot of that going on in Iraq at the time – and won a contract with a telecoms company who were putting the mobile network back into Baghdad. So I started working for them. It was as easy as that, there were contracts flying around like confetti in Iraq in 2003–04.

Mick and Andy's concept was a great one. The security company consisted of a small contingent of Westerners, all ex-Special Forces, and about 2,000 Iraqis, who we trained in bodyguard skills, convoy logistics, site and transit security. We acquired a load of Saddam's old villas, about six or seven of them dotted around Baghdad, as well as some of his old armoured Mercedes. We used the Iraqis as the workforce, while we maintained a low profile. This was essential, because the telecoms company had its HQ in the city's Red Zone, which meant it was considered unsafe.

By contrast, the American contractors would be hanging out of the windows of their vehicles with weapons. They took the view that they should be as conspicuous as possible, which is just the American way. They'd be 'yee-hawing' and high-fiving. This was fine by us, because it meant they drew most of the unwanted attention. Meanwhile, we were driving around in the armoured Mercedes with the blacked-out windows, just like the attackers on the highway. But that way of operating carried risks, because it made us look more local than Western, which meant our biggest threat was actually the Americans. It really was like the Wild West. Actually, it was more like *Mad Max*.

Getting into the Green Zone (the fortified neighbourhood that was home to government buildings, foreign embassies and businesses) wasn't easy, because I spent a lot of time driving around Baghdad on my own, tooled-up with an AK47 and a Glock 19 pistol whilst wearing body armour. Luckily, I still had my ID card from the SBS. I'd drive up to checkpoints, pop my visor down (which had a Union Jack on it) and show them the card. The Americans manning the checkpoints thought we were still serving and would go crazy: 'Fuck, man! We've got Special Forces coming in! Go! Go! Go!' We'd wind the windows back up and laugh our heads off.

The first Thursday working for the company, I said to the guys, 'What's happening tonight?'

'We've got the party.'

'A party? I wasn't expecting that...'

I didn't imagine Baghdad to be much of a party town. As it turned out, every Thursday there was a bash for the telecoms company's employees and our Jordanian partners, who were in charge of recruiting all the manpower. Friday was a non-work day, so everyone would go to this party and get shitfaced. Our job was primarily to look after the clients, but we were allowed to enjoy ourselves.

I turned up to this villa, which was one of Saddam's old places, placed my weapon on the floor, stashed my body armour under my chair, grabbed a beer and waited for the guests to arrive. Everywhere you looked was marble and gold. It was really quite hideous, just as you'd expect a dictator's villa to look. When the first guests knocked on the door, I instinctively reached for my weapon and one of the lads had to tell me to relax. The last time I'd been in Iraq was during Desert Storm, so it took me a while to feel comfortable as an ex-Special Forces soldier in one of Saddam's old villas, with people getting pissed and smoking so much weed you could barely see your hand in front of your face.

The party was beginning to liven up when the door flung open and 13 women wearing burkas filed through. They stepped down into this sunken lounge and, in perfect unison, removed their burkas. There was no verbal command, it was almost choreographed. And now, standing before me, were 13 women in skimpy, brightly coloured lingerie and hooker heels. I'd never seen anything like it in the West, and I certainly didn't expect to see anything like it in Baghdad. Selection interrogation was trippy, but it had nothing on this.

I soon learned that they were Saddam's old prostitutes (we had his old villas, we had his old cars, why not the hookers as well?) and throughout the night they were in and out of bedrooms with our clients. The clients were all shitfaced, and after they'd fallen asleep, the girls would go around the rooms and nick everything they could lay their hands on. They lifted Rolex watches, jewellery and bulging wallets. Some idiot had even left his safe open, with piles of cash inside. That all disappeared. Their last stop was the kitchen, which they cleaned out of food, before putting their burkas back on and leaving. I can't imagine what they'd been through, so good luck to them.

We were taking delivery of piles of weapons and ammunition every day, so we built an army in a heartbeat and had three massive villas interconnected with gun positions on every high point. Whenever we needed to do a logistics move of equipment, we would use locals with connections to the militia to pave our way. The locals would speak to tribal leaders, pay them cash and our convoys would be secured through that district. The operation was seamless, we were bringing in millions of dollars of equipment unhindered and our set-up was the envy of many. We moved on from telecoms and got a job with Schneider Electric, putting the grid back into Iraq. Whenever we moved transformers into the country, I put big sheets over the lorries with 'IRAQI POWER FOR THE IRAQI PEOPLE!' written on them in Arabic. In other words, 'DON'T FUCKING SHOOT!'

The parties continued, each week in a different villa, each week with Saddam's ex-prostitutes going through the same routine. And perhaps not unsurprisingly, complacency began to set in. Brian was a former Special Forces soldier who had gone native. He'd been in Iraq a long time, had dark skin, a big beard and had grown his hair long, so blended in with the locals. He'd also met a local girl called Imam at one of the parties (not one of the prostitutes, I hasten to add) and started a relationship.

Because Brian had been in the SBS a long time, climbed K2 and was a former bodyguard to the Beckhams, he was like a god to the rest of us and we were all a bit in awe of him. One day, Brian came into the compound and asked if he could have some weapons, because he was going to a party in Dora. Dora was a very active neighbourhood of Baghdad and a place to stay away from. I was supposed to be meeting him at the airport the following morning, because I was going on leave and I'd hooked him up with some business people in Indonesia. I reminded him of that, told him to be careful and he shrugged and said, 'Don't worry about me', before waltzing off with his weapons. What I should have said was, 'Mate, don't go, it's too risky.' But that's only with the benefit of hindsight. Brian was an intimidating character and vastly experienced. I thought he'd have his fun and get home safe.

When Brian didn't turn up at the airport, we suspected something bad had happened. It wasn't like him not to be in touch, and not like anyone to not turn up at the airport to get the hell out of that place. But I got on my plane and flew back to London. It was only the following day, while I was sat in a cafe, that I got the dreadful phone call: the Americans had found Brian's body down a backstreet, shot to bits. Apparently, the party he was at had been ambushed by militia, who had heard there were Westerners in attendance. Brian's girlfriend Imam and three other women were slaughtered. But a 15-year-old girl called Sarah survived. She'd been shot through the head, but the bullet had exited without hitting her brain. We managed to get hold of Sarah and put her in a villa, which I suppose was our version of witness protection.

It eventually came out that the police had stormed the party, Brian had made a run for it and been gunned down. When I say 'the police', I mean it in the loosest of senses. There had been a massive recruitment drive and locals would turn up, get uniforms and weapons and disappear into the ether. Often, people you thought were the police were actually militia. Their Glock pistols were supplied by the Americans, and any of the Glocks that didn't end up in the hands of the militia were sold onto the black market, from where we bought them back for the company.

That's what it was like in Iraq at the time, you didn't know if anyone was who they said they were and who was carrying what. Some of the stuff I did and saw could have come straight from the film *Apocalypse Now*. One day, my mate Denny had to pretend I was his hostage to get me through a checkpoint. Denny was dark-skinned, looked quite wild and could have passed for a local. But as funny as we found it, we could have been killed. I'd watch Chinooks coming into the airport carrying pallets of bank notes, piles and piles of them wrapped in cellophane. That was the American way of trying to rebuild the economy, chucking money at everything. But anyone with half a brain could have worked out that if you flood a warzone with money, an awful lot of it will end up in the wrong hands.

I'd read papers and there would be articles complaining about how much the war was costing. But I'd ask myself the question: 'How much is it making the businesses involved in the rebuilding process?' One of the American engineering and construction companies was called KBR, and the joke was that it stood for 'Keep Bush Rich'. The war was a business opportunity for the Americans, a money-making enterprise, which is why it became very difficult for non-US companies to win contracts, including us.

In the end, Sarah's whereabouts were discovered and we received intelligence that there was going to be an attack on our villa, so we got her out to a safehouse in Jordan. We were pushing for legal action to be taken against the police – which was tricky, because nobody knew who the police were – when we heard that Sarah had disappeared. Consequently, the case was thrown out of court because of insufficient evidence. I don't know what became of her.

Brian's death was a terrible shock. I'd worked with him for a long time and he was a close friend. I hadn't lost many friends in the military. There was my mate who died in the parachute accident in Nevada. But when I was in Northern Ireland, and the IRA were trying to blow us up, they didn't get any of us. And it was the same when I was in Iraq as a soldier.

I felt guilty for not having tried to persuade Brian not to go to the party. It would have been a difficult conversation, but had I spoken up, he might still have been alive. Even if he'd told me where to go, at least I could have said I tried. I should have trusted my instincts. Instead, I took the easier option, which was the biggest mistake of my career.

Brian's death was also a major blow for the company, because we'd always wanted to keep a low profile, and now we were all over the news. We were given warnings that if we ever worked on a military contract, there would be consequences from anti-coalition forces. We were looking at such contracts at the time – we also had Iraqis working for us who would have known about it – and an envelope containing a bullet was thrown over the wall of the compound. Also in the envelope was a note written in Arabic, stating that if we didn't stop talking to the Americans, they'd send bullets with our names on.

Brian had become too localised, too blasé and pushed his luck too far. But we were all guilty of that. Being in a warzone takes its toll. We didn't have the support networks we had when we were in the military, or the same umbrella of protection. It reached the stage where I honestly thought I'd leave Iraq in a coffin. The situation in Baghdad was deteriorating. We were hearing stories all the time about people being attacked and convoys being smashed. We had to encase our villas with steel on the inside. When we heard rounds coming close, we had to lock everything down.

It really started kicking off in 2004–05. There was a big price on any Westerner's head and, one day, four of our team got kidnapped. When we were on the phone, trying to negotiate their release, we could hear another guy in the background having his head cut off – the screams, the commotion and the gargling of blood. We got them out eventually, which took money and certain assurances that we'd stop exploring contracts with the Americans. It was horribly stressful and a very surreal situation. But there were lives at stake, so I literally had to block out the background noise. It was no different to fighting in a war: whatever atrocities were going on around me, I had to kick them to the back of my mind and stay focused on the objective.

Another time, I was in the office, typing an email, and a rocket-propelled grenade flew straight past the window and flattened a villa across the road. I looked up momentarily before going back to typing. There were three of us in the office at the time and nobody said a word, flinched or even raised an eyebrow. That's how immune we'd become to all the chaos that was going on around us.

We had Iraqi bodyguards, but I suspected that if the shit hit the fan, their loyalty would only stretch so far. We didn't know who was who, and we knew there were people in our ranks who were dodgy. I slept with a pistol under my pillow and other weapons placed in strategic positions around the room. I'd lie in bed imagining the door being kicked open and the militia storming in. I didn't know what anxiety was, but I was certainly showing some of the symptoms, including panic and uneasiness, which was hardly surprising.

But, like Brian, I got complacent. I started doing things I shouldn't have. I just didn't seem to have any value for my life. We were being paid a fortune, but it was relative to the shit conditions we were living in. Our insurance policies weren't credible, so we had our own policy: if anyone was blown up or shot and badly maimed, we'd shoot each other dead.

I felt a massive sense of guilt at having left my wife and son and was drinking as a coping mechanism, at every opportunity. As soon as I finished work, I hit the bottle. And it wasn't just me – everyone would down tools and get shitfaced in the villa. That was the military culture, and the habits were deep-seated. It was never a light session. It would be gallons of lager and whisky, sometimes dope. Just about anything was available on the streets of Baghdad. I was blacking out almost every night, then waking up the next morning and not being able to remember what had happened the night before. And when you're drinking that much, the visualisation trick doesn't really work. Your mind is confused, it's like trying to navigate in a fog.

Being the boss allowed me to employ pretty much anyone I wanted. So before I knew it, I was surrounded by old mates from the military, mostly lads I served with in the Royal Marines. Having them with me meant being able to have some fun amid the mayhem. One of the lads was called Benny, from Commando training's 576 Troop. Benny was an amazing musician and had a band called Longspoon. He recorded tracks for his new album in Baghdad and we'd listen to him sing on the roof of our villa, while the sun went down, bullets whizzed overhead, explosions went off in the distance and mosques called to prayer. There was one track in particular, 'Symphony of Man', that summed up our situation: 'In the heart of this troubled land, there's a disease, a conflict of man...'

But all the time you're trying to pull that old military trick of having a drink and laughing – or singing – things off, all that chaos compounds in your head. You might not be thinking about it at the time, but it's lurking in a more dangerous place, which is your subconscious. And that just makes you anxious. That's how I met my new friend Valium. Someone recommended it for my anxiety, I bought some off the black market and it quickly became a habit. Before I knew it, I was popping three or four Valium a day, which provided another layer of fog. It put me on a different parallel, where Helen, Luke, home and all of life's harsh realities that I feared terribly didn't exist.

We'd get threat warnings from the US State Department, telling us which areas to steer clear of. Sometimes, there would be a total lockdown. One day, we were told not to leave the building at all, but I wasn't having it. It was my stubbornness coming to the fore again: because I'd been told not to go out, I was determined to go out. I was country manager, I ran the show in Iraq on rotation with another guy, so I thought I could do what I wanted. And, if I'm honest, the threat excited me.

So I told my bodyguards that I wanted to buy a rug. They tried to talk me out of it, but I wasn't budging. It sounds absurd, and it was. We headed to the Al Mansour district in a three-car convoy and when we arrived at the rug shop, I ran straight in and started negotiating with the owner while lying on the floor. I had my body armour on, my MP5 by my side, and I haggled for ages: 'No, no, no, I'm not paying that...' Eventually, I managed to get him down to $2,000. But as I was counting out this big wad of cash, one of the bodyguards came flying through the door. The militia were on their way and it was time to say goodbye.

I paid the money, one of the bodyguards grabbed the rug and we crawled out of the shop. As we were driving off, bullets started coming down the side of the car and a couple flew straight through the rear window. It may sound crazy, but I found it fun. I got a buzz from buying a rug when I wasn't supposed to and having to escape while being shot at. It made me feel alive.

Most people would enjoy the quiet times, but I hated being stuck in my villa doing nothing in particular, just as I hated the downtime in the SBS. I wasn't thinking about the possible consequences of my actions, didn't give a shit. If it happened, it happened. That was my peace in war. I felt so at home in that environment. As crazy as it sounds, dodging bullets, living in fear and banging back Valium to deal with it made a lot more sense than being back in the UK, listening to the incessant chatter of everyday life. I'm sure I would have felt a bit different had I ended up on YouTube having my head sawn off. But I didn't. I'd escaped with my new rug. And a very nice rug it was, too. It now has pride of place on a wall in my house and I smile every time I pass it.

One night, I left a party, jumped in my car and started driving around the city on my own. Nobody ever did that. You were supposed to turn up, get shitfaced and stay overnight at the villa. The Americans were crashing about all over the place, there were bangs going off everywhere, and soon I was hopelessly lost. It was an open invitation to take me hostage. And because I'd forgotten my ID card, even if the Americans had stopped me, I would have been in trouble. I knew I needed to get to a high point, so I could work out where I was. I reached a bridge, opened the door and my AK47 hit the deck, shortly followed by me. Luckily, I wasn't so pissed that I couldn't make out some of the main landmarks below, and I managed to point my car in the right direction and get home.

I was pushing and pushing and pushing, almost begging for some kind of hideous event that would end everything. It was the same situation as when I was a teenager, spiralling out of control. But there was no long arm of the law you could rely on in Baghdad – or Mum – to reach out and stop me.

I'd have moments of clarity and reflection, when I'd conclude that I needed to leave Iraq. But I'd be doing something else stupid a few days later. There were good times in Baghdad, but they were overshadowed by the darkness of my mental state and the drinking. I was out of control, Baghdad was out of control. I don't know how I lasted so long. I don't know how I lasted at all.

15

ONE LAST JOB

elling Helen I wouldn't be coming home had its downsides. I was supporting her and Luke the whole time I was in Iraq, paying the mortgage and the bills, which is what I should have done as a father. When she found a new fella, I was genuinely pleased for her. We were both entitled to new lives and I wanted us both to be happy. However, I phoned Luke once and he addressed me as Matt. I said, 'Luke, this isn't Matt, this is your daddy.' Luke couldn't compute what I was saying, and it convinced me that being in his life would be more confusing and damaging than not being. After 2004, I didn't see Luke, and barely spoke to him, for seven years.

In 2006, I managed to get a divorce, after a long, tortuous process. It happens to so many people in the military. Women can fall in love with the uniform, the macho man of war and the apparent glamour. But there isn't much glamour in being a soldier's wife. Their husbands are away for long periods, during which they have to bring the kids up on their own and maintain the home on not a lot of money. You might be with someone for ten years, then they come out of the military and you suddenly discover that you don't actually like each other. It can quickly curdle into a very resentful relationship and before you know it it's fallen on its arse. Or you might have discovered that while you were still in the military, but thought it was too much hassle to split up, because you'd be heading back to work soon anyway. In moments of clarity I'd think, 'Is this my life? Is this how it's always going to be?' But it's like confronting a cliff face, looming high above you. You feel trapped and helpless.

It was already on the cards to move to Australia with Nat, but the divorce made it a given. Nat was studying psychology, so had a lot of patience with what was going on in my life. She was an angel, the perfect girlfriend. But I wasn't a good boyfriend for long. I'd get off the plane at Brisbane shitfaced and that would be me for the next six weeks. I hated myself and it pains me now to think of the person I was. Not only was I drinking heavily, I was hooked on Valium and had started injecting steroids. What a lethal combination. And when my leave was up, I couldn't wait to get back to Baghdad. Looking back, I can only imagine that Nat couldn't wait to see the back of me, although she insisted that wasn't the case.

Whereas once I'd been a happy drunk, now I was a nasty drunk. I was never one of those soldiers who liked fighting down the pub, but I wasn't able to drink continuously in the military. Now, I'd pick arguments and be verbally aggressive. It wasn't a pretty sight. It reached a point where Nat felt uncomfortable drinking with me, because she knew I would turn. It was horrible for her. And it was horrible for me. The drink was controlling me. It had become my life. Nat did eventually manage to get me off Valium. I came home on leave one time, was searching for my tablets and she'd flushed them down the toilet. It took a horrible few weeks of cold turkey, but with Nat's support I did it.

Nat was my world. I wouldn't socialise with mates while on leave, partly because I was in a strange land, partly because I couldn't be doing with people from the 'normal' world. So I'd do everything with her, and she was undoubtedly a great woman.

However, looking back, I can see I was depressed, dependent and in a world of extreme turmoil. But there was no chance of me speaking to anyone about it. If anyone had suggested I was depressed, I would have told them not to be so stupid. On the surface, my life was brilliant. I was earning loads of money, I had a beautiful house in Australia, a beautiful girlfriend. But my life at home with Nat was as chaotic as my life in Baghdad. There was no safe haven to run to.

I couldn't even stay out of trouble during my occasional getaways to Dubai. Being in Dubai was a massive release, somewhere I could really let my hair down before returning to Australia after a stint in Baghdad. But one night, I was in a hotel bar when a fight kicked off between some Westerners and some locals. I jumped in to try to separate them and got coshed over the back of the head. When I came round, the first thing I saw was my hands in cuffs and my white T-shirt drenched in blood. I looked up to see two Arabs in the front seats, before seeing two Arabs on either side of me. I thought I was back in Iraq and I honestly thought they were taking me away to get my head chopped off. I started thinking about how to get out of the situation – put the cuffs over the driver's head and strangle him, elbow the other two in the neck – before realising I was actually in a cop car in Dubai.

They took me to the hospital and after they'd tested my blood for alcohol and I'd been checked out, I thought they'd let me go. Instead, they took me to the police station. I was going mental, trying to fight them, telling them to fuck off and that I had to catch a flight in hours, but they were having none of it. They threw me in a cell and when I looked round, it was full of Arabs. As it turned out, they looked after me, but I still missed my flight.

I was given one phone call, so rang Nat in Australia and told her what had happened. She managed to get in touch with the Australian foreign ministry, who tried to get involved. The following day, I was frogmarched to my five star hotel room – I had to walk through the foyer with blood-matted hair and wearing my ripped and bloody T-shirt and handcuffs – so that I could give them my passport. When I opened the safe, there was my passport, a big wad of dollars and a bag of diamonds. Why not? Diamond dealing had gone so well the first time. They pocketed my passport, took me back to the cells and eventually let me out later that day. But when I asked for my passport back, they said, 'Not possible, you've got to go to court.'

'What do you mean? I have to go home. Where am I going to stay?'

'Not our problem.'

Later that day, Nat arrived in Dubai. She had no idea I'd been released until she saw me waiting in arrivals. Because I had no idea how long I'd have to stay, I'd booked the cheapest room at the Jumeirah Beach Hotel. But when I arrived, the woman behind reception said, 'Ah, Mr Ollerton, would you please follow me?' We didn't know what the hell was going on. We followed her to this beautiful private reception area, where someone else said to me, 'Sir, we'd like to upgrade you to the presidential suite.' I turned to Nat and said, 'I don't know what the hell is happening, but let's just roll with it...' So that's where we stayed, for the same price as the cheap room. The presidential suite was everything you'd expect it to be. They delivered popcorn to go with the films we were watching, champagne, fruit platters, anything we wanted. And a lot of things we didn't. To this day, I don't know why that happened, but it was yet another one of those silver linings.

The next day, I went to the court and managed to see the judge. I asked him how long it would take for my case to come up, and he said it might take two or three months. Internally I went into a flat spin, picturing the time stretching out before me. Externally I tried to remain calm. I pulled out a wad of cash and said, 'Is there another way?'

'Of course, there's always another way, my friend. You give me six hundred dollars fine and I'll give you your passport back and you can go home.'

So that was that. Not that we went home immediately: we stayed in the presidential suite for four more nights and also managed to get Nat an upgrade to join me in business class on our flight home. It turned out to be one of the best holidays I've ever had.

As good as the money was in Iraq, I knew it could all end in a heartbeat. And I had no problem getting rid of the money I was earning. That created a lot of anxiety. There was work to be done in Baghdad, but the downtime was awful. There were even moments when being dead seemed a lot more comfortable than being alive. I never tried to take my own life and I don't know how close I came to attempting it. But just the fact I was thinking about it was concerning, especially given that I'd visualised so much that had happened in my life. It seemed that suicide would make life simpler for me and everyone around me. I didn't want to be a burden, so I thought maybe I'd drink a bottle of whisky, take a load of pills, quietly pass away and bring the mayhem to an end.

In the end, Nat had enough of me. I came home one Christmas and some furniture had been cleared from the house. My mum was coming to Australia and the bed she was supposed to be sleeping in and the table we were supposed to be eating Christmas dinner on were gone. I don't think Nat did it out of spite, I think she was probably instructed by her friends or family to salvage something from a failed relationship. But Nat was a full-time student and I'd paid for everything in that house, so I went into a rage beyond belief.

But I never stayed upset for long when a relationship ended, I just switched off. I was always able to say, 'Right, that wasn't meant to be, let's move on.' I don't know if that's the military thing of having to lock bad things away and march on, but it's not necessarily a good way to be.

The day after Nat confirmed it was over, I was invited to a baby shower on the Gold Coast. I thought, 'Fuck it, I'll go and have some fun. You meet a lot of women at baby showers...' I always had to have a woman in my life, to the extent that I'd almost always make sure there was an overlap. The thought of being alone scared me, and I was already one day overdue.

I got on the beers big time and met a girl who happened to have exactly the same birthday as me. Sucker that I was, I thought, 'Wow, this was obviously meant to be! She's been sent for you!' Kelly was another Aussie but lived in the States. So the day after spending the night together, we flew to San Francisco. I didn't hang about in those days. Christmas arrived, my mum came over to Australia – all prepared to console me after my recent break-up – and I suddenly had this new girlfriend. Her reaction? 'For fuck's sake...'

My mum tells me now that for years she didn't know me. I was careful not to tell her too much, but she knew enough to know I wasn't right. I kept telling her how wonderful life in Australia was, but she knew that wasn't the case. That Christmas was a nightmare for my poor mum. I was constantly drunk, to the extent I couldn't have a normal conversation. I'd be placid one second and flaring up the next. My mum thought I was suffering from PTSD and advised me to seek help, but I didn't want to hear it. She honestly thought I was going to end up dead. I'd get irritated and tell her she worried too much. But of course she worried, she was my mum.

Because I was still on a temporary visa, I thought I was going to lose my house. I needed a wife. An Australian one. So I proposed to Kelly and she said yes. We got married in a chapel on top of a mountain in Las Vegas and the plan was for her to leave San Francisco and return to Australia to live with me. But I knew deep inside that what I was doing was very, very wrong.

I was having brutal anxiety attacks. My whole body would be numb and shaking uncontrollably and my head would feel like it was going to explode. I actually thought I was going mad, which was terrifying. I seriously thought I was either going to die or end up in a mental hospital. The only way to nullify the anxiety was by drinking, so I was drinking all the time. Anyone with any sense would have said, 'Jesus, this bloke's not right. He's just split up with his girlfriend, he's drinking like a fish and a mental wreck. Maybe I should let him sort himself out before even thinking about marrying him.' Then again, as long as I had a drink, I always managed to do a decent job of seeming happy. So I have to take a lot of the blame. I'd fucked up big time.

Kelly gave up everything to be with me in Australia and all I wanted to do was get out of the relationship. That's when I started thinking a lot about ending it all. One day, I called Nat and told her I'd done something really stupid, that I had nowhere to turn, and that my life was fucked. She told me there was a way out of everything and what I needed to do. Nat had no reason to help me, but she did, and I'll never forget it. She was such an important figure in my life.

Kelly was understandably distraught when I told her it had all been a mistake. She thought she was in this movie romance, but I wasn't the least bit interested. I got myself a Vegas lawyer and got the marriage annulled, à la Britney Spears. And that's when I decided I really needed to leave Iraq.

* * *

But there was one last gig, as there always is. At least in the movies. And it was very nearly the end of me. I took another job working as a personal security detail, part of a four-man ex-pat security team, and we'd taken a VIP to a villa for a meeting. And while the VIP was inside and we were resting up, the compound came under attack. We were used to the sound of gunfire but when the rounds started coming through the gate and a couple of local security guards got shot, we realised the villa, and perhaps the VIP, was the focus. We took cover and when I looked up, I could see that a group of enemy soldiers had taken up positions behind our vehicles, while others were in nearby buildings. We were in danger of getting trapped at the back of the compound and I could feel the situation spiralling out of control. We were already outnumbered, and I knew that we had to act very quickly before reinforcements arrived, which they surely would.

Rounds were fizzing past my head and hitting the wall behind us, but I managed to scramble to my feet, open fire and hit one guy, who went down in a heap. And once the enemy started going down, they stopped coming forward. That gave us the breathing space we needed to be able to do what we needed to do. Amid the mayhem, I somehow managed to formulate a short-term Immediate Action. The first thing you do when you enter a compound is check the floor plan and ascertain your exit routes, besides the main one. That main one was taken by the enemy, but I knew there was one at the rear, if we could trick our attackers. Shaping to move towards the exit on the left-hand side would encourage them to focus their fire on that one spot, allowing us to escape by the other route. So I sent one of our guys over to the false exit and told him to fire sporadically, to give the impression that we were all heading that way.

The enemy fell for the ruse almost immediately. They changed formation in an attempt to dominate that position, and as soon as they did so, another path to our vehicles opened up. We were then able to get into the villa, bundle the VIP into a car and make our escape, while there were still bullets whistling past the windows. It all happened in about 15 minutes, none of our guys was hit and we did the job we were hired to do, which was keep the VIP safe.

I think I was the only ex-Special Forces soldier in our team but the company I was working for only employed ex-military. That being the case, I knew everyone I was working with knew the necessary drills and that when bullets started coming down, they'd follow orders to the letter. When my colleague was sent to the other side of the compound to draw fire, he did it without asking any questions, because he understood its importance. Can you imagine asking someone with no military experience to do that? 'Mate, do you think you could possibly run over there, so that they all start shooting at you?'

You can't plan or practise stuff like that. But when you're as highly trained as I was, solutions come naturally, even in moments of intense pressure. It was because we were all professionals that it all went so smoothly and we were able to achieve our aim. One wrong action by any single person could have led to us all being killed, or having our heads chopped off.

I'm sometimes asked, 'How many people have you killed?' It's a question a lot of soldiers get asked and one we all hate. I prefer to look at it a different way. I don't know if the person I hit in the compound died or not. But if he did, how many people did I save by killing that one person? How many people did I save by opening fire on that car in Fallujah? Had I not, 14 people might have died, including me. I didn't squeeze the trigger because I found it fun. I didn't score the possible kills on the butt of my gun. They could have killed us, so I had to take action. It was the same as being attacked by the chimp. I was close to death in both cases, a small squeeze of a trigger away in the case of the attack in Fallujah, one more bite away in the case of the chimp attack. They were both break points. And the attack on the compound was another one. But I'd had enough of dicing with death by that point. That was the universe saying, 'Fucking hell, is this dickhead still there? GET OUT!'

16

FALSE DAWN

Being in a warzone for six years had almost destroyed my life. By the end, any good memories I might have had of Baghdad had been obliterated. I finally said goodbye to Iraq in 2008. Our contract hadn't been extended, which forced my hand, but I had already started planning my new life in Australia anyway. I was going to gain some knowledge of the property market, invest in real estate, and that would be my new career. This was the external fix that would make all my problems disappear.

I got back with Nat for a bit, split with her again, and was in a new relationship in no time, although this time it was two days overdue. If I'd learned to be on my own, it would have saved so much hassle, so much money and so much time. It was as if I was trading my girlfriends in, I thought it was that easy. What I didn't understand then, but do now, is that Nat was special and not easily replaced.

Sarah had a young son who was the same age as Luke when I left him, which I took as a sign, just as I always thought things were signs when they not always were. Sarah had a drink problem that was worse than mine and beyond anything I'd seen before. I was trying to create a new life for myself away from warzones, find some stability, and I'd found a walking, talking warzone in Brisbane.

One night, I was supposed to introduce Sarah to some friends, but before we got to the bar she was so drunk she could barely talk. I told her I didn't want to be with her and walked away. She didn't come home that night and the following morning I got a call from the hospital. From what I could make out, she'd got in a taxi, tried to do a runner, got into a scuffle, fallen over and banged her head.

I believe that everyone comes into your life for a reason. Even if they're like Sarah and a terrible match, they hopefully direct you to a place where you're happy and content. But Sarah was a harsh lesson. It hammered it home that just because I had a good girlfriend in Nat, that didn't mean the next one would be the same. There's a lot more to relationships than that.

Life away from a warzone wasn't enough for me. Again I found myself not being fulfilled, I needed something more. But I was about to make a bizarre connection that would change all that. A mate called Denny who worked with me in Iraq and now lived down the road from me in Brisbane threw a party, where I met a guy called Simon who used to be in the Intelligence Corps and did a lot of work with the Special Forces. It was fancy dress, but I immediately recognised him as one of my interrogators in Selection, not the fat guy eating sweets, but the one who was yapping around me like a Chihuahua when I first got off the vehicle.

Simon told me about an organisation in Australia he had connections with, called The Grey Man. The Grey Man was set up for the prevention of child prostitution and slavery, primarily in south-east Asia. They would send undercover operatives into brothels, identify child prostitutes and either use local law enforcement to get the kids out or do rescues themselves. Simon thought I could maybe train operatives for them and I was intrigued.

The Grey Man's chief was John Curtis, a former Australian Special Forces Commando. John had a team around him that had been operating in south-east Asia for a number of years. It was all self-funded, but I'd saved some money and wanted to be a part of it. I met some people, put together a package and started doing training around Brisbane. It was awesome, I loved it. I wasn't back on the tools, but I was back in a world that I knew and felt like I was doing something worthwhile.

They asked me if I wanted to go undercover but pretending to be a paedophile felt too raw for me. Then I split up with Sarah and I thought, 'Fuck it, I'm going overseas to do what I said I'd never do.' Vice, the media company, wanted to film the story in Thailand and make a documentary, so I signed up for a trip. But before heading out, I returned to the UK and saw Luke for the first time since he was four.

He was now 11, and it was incredible to see him as a proper grown-up boy. But it was also like seeing one of my best mates again, as if I'd never been away. There was still a lot of work to do in terms of building the relationship into a proper, intimate father and son thing, but it was easier than I thought it would be. For everything I regretted about my relationship with Helen, he was the one bit of goodness that came from it.

When I got to Thailand, I was in holiday mode. There was always an excuse to drink. I'd meet someone and have a beer with them. I'd meet someone else and have a beer with them. And when I wasn't drinking, my anxiety would be crippling, my fear and unease verging on panic.

We were working with the Thai government's anti-human trafficking department (AHTD) in the tourist resort of Pattaya. The plan was to go into bars, identify kids and hopefully come away with photos and video. We'd then meet with the AHTD and plan a bust. But after attending my first briefing, I knew it was a crock of shit. We'd built an intelligence picture and covered a wall with photos of underage girls sold into the sex trade, and I noticed one of the AHTD agents taking pictures of the photos with his phone. In my world, you wouldn't be taking pictures. He didn't need to be taking pictures, so it was a concern to me. I didn't say anything, because we were trying to build relationships, but I knew at that point that this was going nowhere.

The following night, we went in to do the bust. But the first club we went into, the whole staff had changed and they all pleaded ignorance. The problem seemed to be so ingrained in the culture and everything was just so corrupt. We had more busts planned, but I knew they'd be worthless.

One day, we were chilling out on the beach with the crew from Vice. Me and Simon warned them not to go out on the jet skis, because we knew it was a scam run by the local mafia. Tourists would hire a jet ski and when they returned it, the company would claim the clutch was blown or the side had been scratched and keep their deposit. Of course, the Vice team didn't listen to me. One of them had a collision with a boat, did a bit of damage and the beach erupted.

We'd been trying to keep a low profile, and now we needed to get these people out of there quickly. Me and Simon told the others to get back to the hotel as quickly as possible and get ready to leave, because they'd handed over their passport details and hotel information along with the deposit. Meanwhile, me and Simon tried to reason with the jet-ski owner. While that was happening, all these nasty-looking mafia dudes started turning up.

We managed to extricate ourselves from the situation, drifted back to the hotel, got everyone into the cars and as we were driving out of the hotel, the mafia started arriving. We had arranged an emergency RV, which was another hotel called Cabbages and Condoms. Yes, you read that right. When we arrived later that night, having given the mafia the slip, we walked into this hotel and there were condoms everywhere. There was a Father Christmas made out of condoms, condoms hanging from trees, condoms disguised as flowers. And when we left reception, we stumbled upon this perfectly manicured lawn with a spotlight on it, which was covered in little white bunnies, hopping all over the place. Moments earlier, we were being chased by the Thai mafia. I felt like Alice, having fallen down a rabbit hole into Wonderland. Once again, it was a hairy story with a silver lining. And lots of condoms. Exactly where the cabbages came into it, I have no idea.

We did one more bust that night but before long the operation had fallen apart. It became clear that we weren't going to find any solid evidence and the Vice crew said they'd had enough and left. But I was hearing stories about kids being sold to fishermen and raped for days on boats, before being killed and thrown overboard. Whether those stories were true or not, there was certainly a thriving trade in child prostitution in Thailand, and I thought there was more that we could do. I couldn't help thinking that by the time the kids were in the brothels, it was too late. They were earning money, that money was going back home, they had mobile phones and clothes. So the only way to save kids was to find them before they'd reached the brothels.

A guy called Mickey Choothesa ran the Baan Yuu Suk shelter in Chiang Mai, which provided sanctuary and education to vulnerable girls, as well as a charity, the Children's Organisation of Southeast Asia (COSA). There were stories of Mickey carrying kids over the Burmese border while being shot at. He seemed like a proper hero, doing miraculous things, so I thought I'd go up to Chiang Mai and see if I could do anything to help.

I took two guys with me, a former policeman and a former bodyguard, met Mickey and he showed us around the shelter. All the money had been raised through donations and most of it was used to put the kids through school. It was awesome to see all these vulnerable kids getting an education. Mickey told us about the slave camps dotted along the Thai–Burmese border and we decided to try to identify the camps and get some kids out.

After a couple of days at the shelter, we took off in a pickup. I lay on my back, all the way through Thailand, with my bag as a pillow. It was bliss, just staring at the sky, filled with excitement about our mission. We made some connections on the way up to the border and gathered some information about the likely whereabouts of these slave camps, which were really just villages. Our focus wasn't to ask why, but just to get the kids out.

We ventured up into the foothills, which were extremely dangerous. Before we went up, we had to make a decision about whether to take weapons or not. We decided not to, because if we got stopped by a cartel and we had weapons on us, they would assume we were the Drug Enforcement Agency and there could have been all sorts of trouble. It made more sense to pretend to be tourists. All the same, not having a weapon on me made me feel extremely vulnerable. I'd carried weapons on every operation I'd ever done, they were the tools of my trade. The SBS trained us in disarming skills designed specifically for the military and I could have a punch-up, but you don't take a peashooter to a gunfight. If anyone decided to have a pop, we were fucked.

The Thai government supplied villages with medical provisions, but everything was so corrupt, so by the time the provisions got to the people, there might be one bottle of Paracetamol left. So we were trading medical provisions in exchange for information all the way. We were told that one guy would be able to tell us about a village where loads of kids were kept, but when we reached him, he wanted his whole village supplied with medicine. We did as he asked, and he told us that the cartels had been up and interviewed the slave traders, and the plan was for them to return, take the kids away and distribute them to fishing villages and brothels all over the region.

The following day, we went up to the village and found these 22 kids. It was a very tense moment, because we knew the cartel could turn up at any moment and that we had a very limited amount of time to get the kids processed and evacuated to the shelter. Their ages ranged from eight to fourteen. One girl told us that when she found out she was going to be trafficked, she'd run to the nearest police station, told them what was happening, only to be taken to the cells and raped for three days by the policemen and their mates. Luke was 11 at the time, so it was very harrowing to hear stories like that from kids who were about the same age. It made me extremely angry and very passionate about getting those kids out of that situation.

Having processed the kids, we arranged for a team to move them to safehouses over the next few days, before quickly evacuating to another village on the Burmese border. I was on an amazing high that night from believing that I'd done something good. I'd possibly changed those kids' lives, saved them from years of prostitution and an early grave. It gave me a real sense of fulfilment, purpose and belonging. It was like no feeling I'd had before, and I wanted more of it.

That night, we arrived at another village and exchanged more medical products for a room and some food. We had a debrief and discussed our plans for the next few days, in terms of getting the kids to safety. After a well-deserved meal and a couple of shots of Mekhong, we retired to our bamboo huts and hit the hay. I don't know how long I'd been asleep for when I shot up like a bolt. It was dark and I was befuddled. At first, I assumed I'd had a nightmare. Then I heard something going on outside. I peered through the slits in the bamboo and could see armed men arguing with and apparently threatening the villagers. I didn't have to understand Thai to know that the armed men were members of a cartel.

We were in severe danger. We had organised an emergency RV away from the village, but it was too late. There were torches everywhere and if I'd tried to make a run for it, I would have been seen for sure. The alternative was maybe being caught and executed. I drew my knife and hid in the darkest place in the room, behind the door. Had I been hunting for me, it was the first place I would have looked, but it was all I had. The door flew open and nearly hit me in the face. Luckily, it didn't swing back on its hinges, so I remained hidden from view.

A man wielding an AK47 walked into the middle of the room. Sweat was streaming into my eyes and my heart was beating so hard I worried he might be able to hear it. Just as I thought he was going to look behind the door, his mobile pinged. He fished it from his pocket and looked at it for a couple of seconds, before screeching something in Thai – I assume along the lines of 'room clear' – and marching towards the exit. As he left, he looked to his right, and I felt certain he saw me through a gap in the door. I tightened the grip on my knife. But I never had to use it. The man swept back into the village and I made the immediate decision to make my escape under the cover of darkness.

Two of the guys were waiting for me at the RV and we soon found Mickey as well. It transpired that the cartels had discovered that Westerners were in the area and suspected we were working for the DEA, exactly the situation we were keenest to avoid. We didn't sleep that night and at first light slipped out of the village and headed south for our next mission. The journey to safety seemed to go on forever, and we were terrified that danger lurked around every corner. But eventually we made it to safety.

We'd been tipped off about a bar that was run by a Westerner and renowned for using minors for sex, so three of us – me and two Aussies called Tim and Paul – decided to go in undercover. We thought that if we went in separately and pretended not to know each other, we'd be able to spread our net wider. The brief was to keep a low profile and get as much information as we could, including details about the owner and footage of the rooms upstairs, where sex with children was alleged to take place.

It was all going to plan. I'd identified the owner, who was a cockney, and was minding my own business in the corner of the bar. But I soon got chatting to the owner, one drink turned into a few, which turned into a few more. Before I knew it, I was being 'introduced' to my two mates and I was part of the gang. By the end of the night, I'd got involved in a one-armed press-up competition in the middle of the bar, Tim was playing the drums, Paul was on the mic singing karaoke and we were best mates with everyone.

As mad as it sounds, that was the best way to do it, rather than skulking in the corner nursing a glass of lemonade, peering over the top of a book. Everyone was pissed, so we had to get pissed too. 'Lemonade?! This is a Thai sex bar!' We managed to create enough of a smokescreen that Paul was able to get upstairs and look at the rooms, which contained no kids, but did have CCTV connected to a central control room full of TV screens.

Then The Grey Man made a wrong move. While we were still in Thailand, they told the media that we'd just rescued 22 kids from being trafficked. By that time, The Grey Man had done 140-odd such rescues in south-east Asia, but to get 22 kids out in one hit was a big deal. The story spread like wildfire, and I think the US State Department got hold of the story, contacted the Thai government and said something along the lines of, 'What the hell is going on? We give you millions of dollars a year to prevent the trafficking of children, and we're reading that a four-man team has done more than you've ever done.' The Thais immediately went on the defence, which quickly turned into attack.

They savaged our credibility. They claimed that The Grey Man was a crooked organisation, conning donors out of money, which was then lining our pockets. They also claimed that the 22 kids hadn't been sold into slavery at all. That story quickly became accepted fact and suddenly we were being hunted down. We were ignorant of all the controversy, so headed off to do another operation. But had we been seen by the wrong people, we would have been arrested.

Shortly afterwards, news reached us that the Thai police were hunting us down and we needed to get out of Dodge, quickly. A disgruntled former Grey Man operative had started working for the AHTD, so we were concerned that he might have passed on our names, and if they had caught us and asked for papers, we would have been in the shit. But we managed to escape over the border and into Burma, before flying back to Australia.

Not long after that, and against my better judgement, I got back together with Sarah. I was staying on the Gold Coast with her family when my phone started pinging with text messages from people telling me to buy a newspaper. The first thing I saw when I walked into the newsagent was a picture of me, my Grey Man colleagues and the 22 kids we'd rescued, on the front page of *The Australian*. Luckily, our eyes were blacked out. Not so luckily, the story contained more claims that The Grey Man was a bogus charity. And the story wasn't just in *The Australian*, it was in every major newspaper in the country, as well as being all over the TV news.

I immediately knew that The Grey Man would soon be no more. I knew that the majority of the donations went straight to the kids and that none of us took a salary. But the stories claimed that money was being misused. They also claimed that the kids we had rescued were living perfectly normal lives with their families. What else were they going to say to journalists who stuck recorders under their noses? They relied on the Thai authorities for financial and medical support. Everything was being denied at every level. Even other charities waded in, backing up the Thai government's claims.

It was devastating on a personal level. I'd got my teeth into something that really mattered to me and now it was being rubbished in a very public way. I'd also spent all my savings on The Grey Man, so my whole world dropped away beneath me in a heartbeat. But it was also gut-wrenching to know that with The Grey Man gone, so many kids would suffer as a result.

Whatever mistakes John Curtis made – and it was him that came in for most of the flak – I knew his organisation had done a lot of good things for a lot of people. But the culture of child prostitution was just so ingrained, which meant any charity trying to do anything about it was swimming against a very strong tide. You can try to be a superhero, fly in and try to change things, but only the Thais themselves have the power to change their own culture.

17

HAPPY NOW?

thought Sarah and I could make things work, but the old issues soon reappeared. As soon as she saw stories about The Grey Man she said, 'I knew what you were doing out there was a load of shit.' She'd take great pleasure in letting me know that anything that meant a lot to me meant nothing to her. She just wanted me to get a bog-standard job and be at home the rest of the time. And whenever someone says to you, 'Why don't you just grow up and get a proper job, like a normal man would do?' you know that comes from jealousy. That's them trying to drag you down into their own unfulfilling lives.

For a while when I was living with Sarah, I worked in a laundrette. There's nothing wrong with working in a laundrette, it's just not my scene. But that's how under pressure I was to live this 'normal' life. And the pressure didn't just come from Sarah. After returning from Thailand, I kept telling myself that I needed to keep myself safe. And part of that was having an everyday job. Eventually Sarah and I parted for good, I started putting myself out there and landed a job with a large oil and gas company.

I moved into a beautiful bachelor pad in an old wharf on the Brisbane River and it was the first time I'd ever really been single. It was the best thing I ever did and for a while life seemed like absolute bliss. I should have tried it more often.

Too often, people look externally for purpose and content-ment. I learned that I didn't need anyone else in my life, that my purpose and contentment came from within. I think that dependence on other people stemmed from my time in the military. But even in the military, you need to make sure your own shit is together before worrying about other people. Because if you have your own shit together, you're in a better position to look after other people anyway. No one can rely on you if you're broken.

I was a project manager for all the wells across Queensland. It paid good money, it gave me a certain amount of autonomy and, from the outside looking in, it seemed like a dream gig. But I couldn't stand it. Spending so much time in an office was a nightmare, to the extent that I was in the gym three times a day. I don't think I'd ever been fitter. Working in an office, doing mundane work for a company I cared nothing for, wasn't where I was destined to be. It had no meaningful purpose, just as being a mercenary in Iraq – which is exactly what I was – had no mean-ingful purpose.

However, that period did help me get back on track, because it gave me a routine and some stability, for maybe the first time ever. I started thinking about how I'd managed to change my life in the past. I thought about joining the Royal Marines, Special Forces Selection and about the attack in Fallujah, when I was able to change my situation through the power of positive thinking. I used to say to myself every day: 'I am willing to accept change, and as difficult as it may seem, I know it will lead to bigger and better things.' It was difficult at times, because I was still drinking to excess, but I could feel change coming, even if I didn't know where that change would take me. It was around that time that I finally worked out that *I* wasn't the problem. So many people must think that way: if I'm not happy working in an office and doing a boring job that pays me the money to support my family and pay my bills, then there must be something wrong with me. I'd almost resigned myself to believing I'd just have to deal with being discontent for the rest of my life. But I simply hadn't found my calling. There was something out there that would satisfy me and give me purpose. I didn't have to sit behind a desk, wearing a suit and pushing paper for the rest of my working days.

I kind of wanted another girlfriend, but the fact I couldn't find one was maybe another sign that major change was afoot. I had a number of female friends and was seeing a 24-year-old at one point, whose dad was the same age as me. Holly was nice, but nothing serious. My contract with the oil and gas company was coming to an end and there was nothing on the horizon, so it was almost as if I was being forced out of the country. But despite all this, I kept clinging on like a limpet.

One night, I had an argument with Holly and went down the gym to let off some steam. After the session, I was heading home on my bike when I reached a junction just outside the gym and a car smashed straight into me. I was splattered on the deck, my handlebars were all twisted and my knee was in agony. The guy jumped out of the car and was very apologetic, but it turned out he only had one eye, so that when he turned right he didn't see me. That was another nudge towards the exit, although the universe wanted me to go out in an even greater blaze of ignominy.

I had some time off work but a few weeks later was ready to go back to the gym. I used to do these workout routines and my favourite was called Murph, which was named after a Navy SEAL called Michael Murphy, who received the Medal of Honor for his actions in Afghanistan. Murph consisted of a mile run, 100 pull-ups, 200 press-ups, 300 squats and another mile at the end, all while wearing a 20-pound weight vest. There'd be a few of us tackling Murph at any one time and we'd race each other.

My first time back at the gym, I headed out the door for my second mile run and went screaming down the road, because I was desperate to beat my personal best. I could feel a rival breathing down my neck, and I was muttering, 'I must win this' over and over again. About 100 metres from the finish, I ducked down the pavement side of a rubbish truck and the bin-collecting sidearm punched out and knocked me straight through a garden fence, on exactly the same spot I'd been hit by the one-eyed dude. There was a bit of damage – and I didn't win the bloody race! – but I was more in shock. I could have pressed charges against the one-eyed dude and the owner of the dustcart but decided not to. They didn't do it on purpose, and they might have lost their jobs, been unable to provide for their families and it would have been a lot of hassle for me. And that was the moment it finally sunk in: 'Ollie, you idiot, how many hints do you want? Get it into your thick skull that you need to fucking leave…'

People always used to laugh at the fact that I'd get myself into loads of shit and come up smelling of roses. I even managed to find the positives in being run over twice in the same place in the space of a few weeks. Instead of thinking, 'What a pain in the arse', I thought, 'It could have been so much worse.' Not only that, I thought, 'Why has this happened? Is this a sign that I need to make changes?' I do believe in fate, but I also believe we define our own destinies. Everything is there for us, we just have to line ourselves up for the opportunities.

The company I was working for had some former fighter pilots in for a corporate training day, which was actually pretty useful. But I was also sitting there thinking, 'These people worked in jet planes up at 12,000 feet. Maybe they can teach CEOs a thing or two, but how relatable is this to real life? Imagine if you tried to teach people from the corporate world Special Forces skills. That makes far more sense.' Then one day, I was flying across an oil field, staring out of the window at this great expanse below, and the solution opened up before me. I imagined a load of civilians from the corporate world doing a simulated escape and evasion exercise across the terrain. I imagined veterans, guys suffering with PTSD, working as instructors, teaching Special Forces lessons – both physical and mental – to people wanting to better themselves. It seemed almost real.

I'd got so much satisfaction from helping people through The Grey Man organisation, and that had created a spark, a passion to improve people's lives. It's an innate thing in most humans to want to help others. And I realised that helping other people was my therapy and my forte. For the first time in my life I had a clear idea about who I was and what I wanted, and that was something I stumbled upon in the wilds of Thailand. It was suddenly all so clear in my mind. That moment on the plane was a daydream but also the skeleton of a business plan. It was a moment of great clarity, an epiphany of sorts.

One thing I said I'd never do was go back to the UK, where there were too many bad memories and there was too much upset and trauma. But one Thursday morning, I suddenly woke up at 3am and thought, 'Why don't I go home?' And as soon as I opened the doors of possibility, everything started flowing. It was like an energy came flooding in and suddenly I had answers. I put almost everything I owned on Gumtree, cleared the flat and was gone in a couple of weeks, flying out on 11 July 2014.

My brother had landed a job as a helicopter pilot for Shell in Malaysia, which meant we'd miss each other again. Because we'd both been in the military and off here, there and everywhere, we'd hardly seen each other for 20-odd years, so him clearing off just as I was coming home was a blow. But, once again, there was a silver lining. Mum was moving into his house in Cornwall, which meant there was a spare house for me to live in.

When I arrived back in the UK, all I could think about was my business plan, day and night, to the extent that I was even dreaming about it. But I needed money, so I soon got sucked back onto the circuit. A guy I was in the military with got me a job in surveillance, chasing Russian crooks around London. They were businessmen, worth billions, involved in corruption. We'd follow them everywhere, spying on who they were meeting, taking photographs, even following them to airports and then to Switzerland, where we'd continue operations. The intelligence was fed back to the company, which was then fed back to solicitors, who were working on behalf of clients. I had a job and I had money, but it wasn't my passion and it did nothing for me.

It was about this time that I told my brother about my business plans, which he fully supported. Justin also loaned me some money. He said to me, 'You're like that bloke Bourne – except you're Broke Bourne.' On 11 October 2014, I quit the surveillance job. And on my way down to Cornwall, I met up with Foxy at a service station on the M40. We'd served together in the Marines, but he was only a support rank at the time, nothing more than a bit of skin. Still, he was one of my best mates and I loved hanging out with him, mainly because we shared the same warped sense of humour and loved the same music. But I hadn't seen him for 13 years and didn't even know he'd done Selection and been in the SBS. After I left the military, I severed ties with pretty much everyone I'd served with. I didn't really have any friends outside of whichever relationship I was in at the time, which is quite unusual for an ex-soldier. I was trying to find an alternative, something new, and I thought that meant completely forgetting the past and focusing on the future. The upshot of that thinking was bouncing all over the world, searching for that fix, when I should have been looking inside myself. But when you sink into a depression – even if you don't know you're depressed – you hide yourself away from the people you were close to. That's not a wise thing to do, because they're the people who know you best and are best placed to help.

After a couple of coffees, me and Foxy checked into a hotel and got on the lash, big time. When Foxy left the SBS, he went down a similar route to me and ended up working for a global facilities management company. It wasn't his thing, but he thought it was expected of him. And when I told Foxy all about the plan for my business, which I was already referring to as Break-Point, it turned out that he'd been thinking along similar lines. We talked all night, visualising in forensic detail what the business would look like, and from that moment on, I decided not to work for anyone else full-time.

In Cornwall, I virtually locked myself away for two months. I'd get up in the morning, do some exercise, meditate and visualise the life I wanted. When I was still in Australia, I'd learned meditation from a spiritual psychologist. It gave me the ability to clear my mind, stop the chatter and focus. People get freaked out when they hear the word 'meditation', but there's nothing mysterious about it. It's the mental equivalent of tidying up a room or chucking out a load of possessions you don't really need. Meditation is about keeping your head in a battle-ready state and clearing a path. You don't have to sit there in the lotus position, making a humming noise. You can just sit in an armchair, close your eyes, concentrate on your breathing, clear the mind and focus on the things that are really important to you.

People can solve a lot of issues with meditation. It certainly put me on the right track. But because the value of meditation isn't immediately tangible, it's hard for people to understand. Meditation's rewards take time, sometimes a lot of it. It's almost like planting a tree and waiting for the fruit to grow. Most people don't have the patience for that, they need to see fully formed fruit immediately. For a long time, you might only see subtle changes in your lifestyle or view of the world. But if you take short-cuts all the way through your life and you're not battle-ready, when the shit hits the fan, you won't be able to deal with it and things will get worse. The older you get, the more things compound. Your mind becomes almost impenetrable, so that you need a jackhammer rather than a feather duster to clean it out.

During my self-imposed imprisonment in Cornwall, I might listen to the radio while I was cooking my food at night, but I'd never have the TV on. I basically created a boot camp for myself and tried just about every suggestive trick possible. I listened to inspirational podcasts. I made lists of things I wanted to change. I drew a clock face, wrote a different goal at each number and visualised achieving that goal. I stood in front of the mirror every morning and read a contract to myself, outlining what I needed to do to succeed in business. It felt unnatural and I found it really uncomfortable, but if you can't tell yourself what you want, how can you hope to achieve it?

I also visualised myself on stage with Foxy, in front of a big audience, talking about our time in the Special Forces. I imagined what we'd be wearing, who was there, the questions that were being asked. And every time we stepped onto that stage, we would get a rapturous reception. That time in lockdown was like a religious mania. It had worked before, it would work again.

There were times when I doubted my ambition and methods, because I kept hitting brick walls. I couldn't get my hands on any cash, because I didn't have a credit rating in the UK. In the end, my mum had to get me a credit card. I was 43 years old at the time, which was quite sobering. Even with my mum's help, it was a struggle. I had a bit of work, doing hostile environment awareness training a couple of times a month, which gave me just enough money to live on. But it costs a lot to start a business. I needed to get a website built and money for marketing. I'd told Foxy I was going to get it all sorted, but it was getting to the point where I wasn't going to get my house rent-free and I might have to go back onto the circuit, which would have been disastrous.

My drinking was still out of control, which was another major problem. I would go periods without it, but any excuse to get back on it, I'd take it. Foxy likes a drink, but I would carry on after him. I'd leave the pub, go to the train station, buy a load of beer and drink it all the way back home. Even drinking for one night would have a detrimental effect. It would change the chemistry, dilute my passion, stop me from wanting to train and make me depressed. It would cloud my vision and obliterate days that I couldn't afford to lose.

In a bid to control my drinking, I went and had acupuncture. I was willing to do anything it took, and I managed to confine the drinking to weekends. I told my mum about my plans and she shared my passion. Between my late teens and my early forties, I'd barely seen her, which was another reason I wanted to come home. I started to worry that something might happen to me while I was away and I wanted to spend more time with her, especially as she had supported me so much. She had taken an out-of-control boy, sent him down the right path, shared his ambitions and supported him when he was going through the wringer. But not everyone stood so squarely behind me when I was trying to get Break-Point off the ground.

A close family member advised me not to indulge my dreams. He pointed out that other people were already doing the same thing, that it was a crowded market and I was wasting my time. He said I should do what I knew best, what everyone from the Special Forces does, and what brings in plenty of money: get back on the circuit, do VIP security, surveillance, all the stuff I'd done and hated.

He didn't mean any harm, he was just trying to protect me. I thank him for that. But there's nothing worse than someone pissing on your fire. And more dreams are extinguished by people close to you than anyone else, because they're the people whose opinions you respect the most. I walked away from that conversation with major doubts and my passion dimmed. But before long, I was reinvigorated. Like my old maths teacher, the careers officer and my old Royal Marines sergeant, he'd done me a favour.

At the beginning of 2015, I did some hostile environment awareness work at Pippingford Park, in Sussex's Ashdown Forest. And as soon as I got on that land, I thought, 'This is Break-Point.' I just felt so at home. I looked at the company's offices and thought, 'I will be in those offices, that's where Break-Point will operate from.' It was time to work my magic.

The blueprint was almost complete, the website was being built, I was looking into making pitches to corporates and I had what I thought was an HQ. But as hard as I tried to make things happen, I just couldn't. I'd been visualising more intensely than ever, so I couldn't understand it. It even made me doubt whether the attack in Fallujah had meant anything at all. To make matters worse, I was quickly running out of money and surrounded by people telling me to get a 'real' job.

Then one day, I got a call from Foxy.

'Mate, you know that idea we've got for Break-Point? How do you feel about doing that on TV?'

'Shut the fuck up. Have you been drinking?'

'No, I'm sitting here with the production company. If you're interested, you can have a chat with them now.'

The guy from Minnow Productions told me that they'd already built the treatment for the show and asked if I'd be up for appearing on it. It took me about half a second to say yes. It was as if someone or something had suddenly said, 'Enough! Here's what you wanted. Happy now?'

I'd had to take a deep breath and withdraw from the world in order to clear all the shit out of the way and move forward again. But now I'd finally delivered. Visualising rewards had long been a key part of my thought process, whether it was beers with my mates after Special Forces Selection or cocktails on a beach with the missus after a particularly gruelling mission. And this TV show was my reward. It was the stage I had visualised, except a hundred times bigger. It was the perfect platform, the exposure I'd been seeking.

I'm aware that people will be sceptical, but I actually believe that if I put enough effort into visualising something, it will happen. Opportunities will begin to arise that will enable you to realise your ambitions. But it's not voodoo. It's not simply a case of saying, 'I want to be a millionaire', over and over again, and seeing the money flood in. It's about painting a picture of how that money will improve your life, which involves emotion, which in turn makes you motivated enough to follow your dream. And I truly believe that because I painted the picture of my business in such minute detail, and attached so much emotion to it, it delivered so much more.

18

WHO DARES WINS

he idea for the TV programme had already been pitched to a few ex-Special Forces guys but they had turned it down. People from the Special Forces aren't supposed to be celebrities and a lot of people from that world wouldn't dream of revealing their identities. A lot of former Special Forces guys had conducted sensitive operations globally and were still apprehensive about possible repercussions. Also, once you show your face, you can't go back to the circuit and that comfortable old world of security and surveillance. But for me and Foxy, it was the perfect opportunity, because we wanted to leave that old world behind for good. So just seven months after returning from Australia with nothing but a dream and a bag full of clothes, I signed a contract to appear in series one of *SAS: Who Dares Wins*.

The producers had sourced everything for the show from the internet, which was important for me and the other DS. The only way the Ministry of Defence would have accepted us taking part was if we were seen not to be providing them with insider information. However, we would still have an input, so there was a strange dance between us and the programme makers. They built the framework, which was 30 guys being put through an approximation of Special Forces Selection for eight days, and we filled in some details. So if we felt something wasn't appropriate, we'd tell them and they'd invariably listen.

We knew that everything we did and said would be scrutinised by the MOD before it was broadcast, but we had no intention of revealing any secrets. The show was never supposed to be about operations or tactics, it was purely about giving a glimpse of the physical and mental demands of Selection. And Selection doesn't teach you to be a Special Forces soldier, it merely prepares you to be trained as a Special Forces soldier. The applicants weren't going to be in the SAS or SBS after eight days on the programme, the plan was simply to beast them, to find out if they had the raw minerals for Selection.

There were some Special Forces veterans who said, 'This isn't the sort of thing ex-Special Forces should be doing, it's not on.' But I knew we weren't going to divulge any of our dark arts, so the only people we'd be compromising was ourselves. Does the programme take away from the mystique of the Special Forces? Maybe. Prior to *SAS: Who Dares Wins*, the only Special Forces soldiers most people had seen were Andy McNab in silhouette form and the chaps storming the Iranian Embassy in 1980.

While I understood why we had to be secretive, I thought it would be more beneficial to remove the masks and come across as real people, with the same issues as everyone else. That doesn't make the Special Forces any less effective in war. It's not as if the enemy will be watching the show and thinking, 'Brilliant, these boys aren't as hard as we thought they were.'

It comes down to ego, people wanting to maintain the mystique so that other people think they're something they're not. But most of all, I thought the show would allow veterans, regardless of their rank, to be proud of what they'd done for the country. And I think it's done that. Veterans aren't celebrated here like they are in America. Too often in Britain, veterans are ignored.

Shortly after signing the contract, I phoned Helen, because I thought Luke needed to know that I was going to be on TV. I told her what the programme would involve, that we were going to take civilians and give them a taste of the hardest military selection process in the world, and she replied, 'So why do they want you?'

'Helen, I did Special Forces Selection twice.'

'Well, you never told me anything...'

When I appeared on TV for the first time, I had people contacting me and saying, 'I knew it! You used to disappear for ages and no one would know where you'd gone. Either you were in the Special Forces or in and out of prison!'

The recruits were just random people, selected by the programme makers and handed to us in Pembrokeshire. We had no idea who they were, but it was our job to find out their stories and try to crack them. What they all had in common was that they wanted to prove something to themselves.

Society makes everything soft for people these days. There are few things in everyday life to test people's fortitude. The warrior urge is deeply ingrained in a lot of people, especially men. For thousands of years, war was the norm. Only for a short speck of history has war been unusual. For 90 per cent of human history, people hunted and were hunted, which meant fighting for survival on a daily basis, which gave people a meaningful purpose. But today, so many people have no outlet for those instincts. I think that's why there is so much anger in society, because people are not able to release it.

Whenever I've had periods with no meaningful purpose, I've spiralled out of control. Life will find a purpose for you, whether you like it or not. And if you don't choose your own destiny, there's a chance you might channel that pent-up energy into crime or end up doing a job in an office that you hate with every ounce of your being, essentially marking time until you die. Strange as it sounds, I used to see civilians living in warzones and think they were living a more natural existence than someone sitting behind a desk for nine hours a day, existing in a hazy world of nothingness. They wouldn't choose to be in a warzone, but at least their life had meaning, however horrible their situation.

A few generations ago, far more men did manual labour, whether they were working down a pit, on a farm or in a steel plant. Those men led tough, tough lives. They were tested, both physically and mentally, every day. They plodded through life – got up at the crack of dawn, walked to work, worked like a dog for nine hours, walked home again, had dinner, fell into bed, and repeated that routine every day until they retired. They didn't have time to think about their mental state. They were too busy struggling to put food on the table and heat their homes, and they didn't know anything different. But far fewer people do such grinding work nowadays. Instead, people are fed into the system like coins into a machine, and they sit in offices, expending no energy and staring out of windows feeling frustrated and depressed with their lives.

So many people don't focus on the things they want in life. They don't have a plan, because they don't have any goals. And if you don't have any goals or a plan, you lack any drive, which can lead to mental health issues. I don't understand why people are so surprised that mental illness has become so prevalent in Western society. If you have no meaningful purpose, year after year, you start to close down. It's almost like your brain saying, 'If you're not going to use me, I might as well pull down the shutters.'

Some people go to the gym and train all day long, but never even think about training their brains. That's a metaphor for the flimsiness of much of modern life. People assume that if something looks good from the outside, then it must be sound. It's about selling a perception of perfection, not the reality. It's the same with social media. It's all pictures of perfect families on holiday in Disneyland. Nobody ever posts on Facebook that they got hammered at the weekend and did a shit in the middle of the lounge, just as I didn't tell anyone that I urinated all over my wife's prized possessions. Deep down, that person posting the picture of their holiday in Disneyland might be suffering inside, because they don't know who they are or why they're here.

A lot of the guys we got on *SAS: Who Dares Wins* flirted with joining the military before going down a different path, or had no interest as young men but developed an interest when any chance of joining the military had passed. But the basic premise of the programme was to see if you can take someone with no military experience, give them a taste of Selection and see if they have the makings of a Special Forces soldier. It turned out that most of them didn't.

They might have thought they were gagging for a taste of the warrior life, to meet a need inside of them, but it was too much of a shock for them. Once we took away their everyday comforts, they disintegrated before our eyes. These were people who could lift massive weights in the gym and run for miles. But they were also people who worked behind a desk and had never even been on a camping holiday. They were used to eating when they wanted to, sleeping when they wanted to and being warm pretty much all of the time.

It made me wonder what would happen if this country ever went to war and had to introduce conscription. I reckon it would be mayhem. The general fitness of the conscripts would be OK, but finding people of credible character, who could handle the indignities and the hardship, would be far more difficult. I some-times think about the boys who fought for the United States in the Vietnam War. One minute they were at college, the next they were dropped into the middle of the jungle and seeing their mates being blown up or killed by some primitive animal trap. I wanted to be a soldier, wanted to be on the frontline, but those boys had no choice. Going from a normal life to a warzone would make people crumble in a heartbeat, especially today, when most people don't know what hardship is.

There was a guy from that first series who was a fitness instructor and apparently training to be a stuntman. On the face of it, he had some of the attributes of a Special Forces soldier. But while we were waiting for the recruits to turn up on the first day, we were getting reports from our mole that this guy was marching up and down the train in the boots we'd sent him, running his mouth off about the show, while wearing a skimpy vest and a compass around his neck. This despite the fact he'd been given clear instructions not to talk about where he was going and what he'd be doing.

Sure enough, when this guy turned up, he was a typical show pony with a massive ego. From the moment he stepped off the train, he had our backs up. He kept talking about how he was going to smash this and that, about his exploits as a martial artist and an endurance athlete. He had the biggest guns, no doubt had his pick of the girls and probably thought he'd take the other recruits to the cleaners. Being an alpha male isn't necessarily a bad thing in the Special Forces, if you can control it. But this guy strug-gled to control it. He was ultra-competitive and had a problem with authority, and as far as the DS were concerned, his attitude made him a potential weak link.

Either people like that change very quickly during Selection or they fall apart. As it turned out, we managed to push him and push him and quell his ego. But every now and again it would reappear. He didn't know he was doing it until after he had done it. And when he did, you'd see the look of acknowledgement in his face: 'Oh shit, I'm being a twat again...'

This guy's fellow recruits quickly became pissed off with him, because his constant need to gob off was making life tougher for them. In the military, you don't deal with things on an individual basis, because you haven't got time to take people aside and give them one-on-one coaching. Instead you have to say, 'Right, you're all getting punished today, because of number ten.'

As DS, it was our job to pounce on the show ponies and chop their heads off if they were getting above their station, because those kinds of people can corrupt the group. They can also be dangerous. Being humble and grounded is a very important trait for a Special Forces soldier to have. On some missions, you have to be aggressive. But most of the time, Special Forces soldiers operate under the radar. It's not about hitting a target, smashing the place up and posting it on Instagram. It's a lot more serene than that. And if you do get taken hostage and start mouthing off, you're quite likely to end up with a bullet in the head. It might also result in your mates being killed and your mission being blown.

The first two days, the group were like a herd of wild horses, some of them wilder than others. It was our job to tame the egotists, not allow anyone to do his own thing on the fringes, and create a tight-knit pack. You can't have rogue elements in combat situations, you must be a solid unit, working as a team. Once you've created that solid unit, camaraderie follows. And a good team will either rally round any remaining egotists and help to change them or they will ostracise them. It's almost like natural selection.

After escape and evasion, this guy threw in the towel. Him and another recruit got lost and we had to hunt them down the next day. The plan was to hood and reinsert them, but this guy was on his knees saying he didn't want to go on. Not only that, he was trying to talk his mate into quitting. And when someone is that tired, it's not hard to persuade them to chuck it all in. That made me so angry. If you want to throw in the towel, that's fine. But trying to persuade someone else to throw in the towel, because it would make you feel better about your failure, is not on. It's the equivalent of someone on the battlefield saying, 'Stay with me and get shot', rather than, 'Go on without me.'

I got this guy out of the car and unloaded on him, told him what a piece of shit he was for trying to corrupt a fellow recruit. He handed me his number, which meant he had voluntarily withdrawn, and I took great satisfaction from taking it from him. But the production company got wind of it and wanted him back in, because he made for good TV. So the decision was overturned, this guy was put back in and nothing was mentioned about the episode when the programme was broadcast. That irritated me, although the thought of the horrors that still awaited him in the process placated me somewhat.

Anything that isn't a bit of a struggle to make can't possibly be any good, so me and the other DS are always rubbing up against the programme makers. There will be times when they try to push their ideas onto us and we simply won't have it, but that's simply part of the creative process. As it turned out, this guy made it to the final five, which actually gave me a lot of pleasure. In only eight days, we'd taught him that his ego was his biggest enemy and refined him as a person. I'm convinced that being on the programme changed him for the better, and he's actually become a good friend.

Another important aspect of the show is the success of the underdog. It's not always the fittest, strongest and fastest people who prevail, often it will be someone who has flown under the radar for most of the week and we've barely noticed. Ryan Roddy, from that first series, was that kind of character, the perfect grey man.

Ryan had had a tough upbringing in Northern Ireland, was phenomenally fit, a great team player and humble. While some people were telling everyone within earshot how great they were, Ryan was plodding along in the pack, saying nothing. And when you're dealing with someone who is humble, you automatically have far more respect for them. I wasn't surprised when Ryan was one of the last men standing at the end of the series.

Amuz Sandhu, who appeared in series three in Morocco, had only recently beaten cancer and a consequent alcohol addiction. He had this fire inside of him, and I think that came from believing he might die. After day one, all of the DS were doubting him, but he proved us wrong. Amuz would be in tears, seemingly in agony, but he'd keep putting one foot in front of the other. In the end, we were calling him 'Cyclone', because he was like a slow-moving depression. Amuz is the kind of person you want in a warzone, someone who will keep moving forward, even when the chips are down and they are at their lowest ebb. That means a lot more than someone grandstanding at the front of a march and finishing first in the sprints.

In the most recent series, there was a guy called Milo Mackin who also fitted the bill of the grey man. He was a fit lad who had flirted with joining the military, but he was also quite subdued. His brother Travis was killed by an IED in Afghanistan when he was only 22. And because his other brother Corbin was also serving at the time, Milo didn't pursue his military dreams for the sake of his family. But Milo was desperate to do Travis proud. And from that quiet, unassuming lad, he blossomed as the week went on. Milo's development curve was very steep and he was one of only three recruits standing at the end.

We live in a society in which the extrovert, the boaster and anyone who makes the most noise is thought to be the most likely to succeed. But that's not the Special Forces way. The bigger the ego, the bigger the insecurity. Most Special Forces soldiers don't tell the world what they've done. It's enough that they know what they've done, having taken themselves to their absolute limits.

19

JUST LIKE YOU

The programme makers were extremely clever in creating a show that wasn't just about the military and the physical attributes of soldiers, but also about human psychology. That made it appeal to a far wider audience. It meant that people who didn't have any interest in the military watched it and got caught up in the emotional turmoil of the recruits, and particularly their backstories, some of which were brutal. They could relate to those stories far more than the sight of a man yomping across a hill with a big pack on his back.

The recruits' backstories include bereavement, personal illness, bullying, rape and murder, as well as more universal themes such as failure and redemption. These are stories that resonate with so many viewers. One of the show's appeals is seeing people achieve amazing things despite adversity. That's inspirational to everyone. Humans want to see fellow humans surpass expectations, unless you're one of those bitter, jealous people who feels threatened by other people overcoming obstacles and succeeding in life.

It was really important to me that I demonstrated the various stunts, rather than gobbing off and asking the recruits to do stuff I can't – or simply don't want to do – myself. People sometimes say to me, 'I see you got the short straw again, having to stand in that icy water or abseil down the cliff face.' But that's not the case at all; it's far better to actually demonstrate to people the calibre of soldiers we were and still are. I also just love doing it, it makes me feel alive. Although my enthusiasm did almost kill me during the second series in Ecuador.

None of us had done helo drills for years, because it's not the sort of thing you do on Civvy Street. Me and another DS on the show, Mark 'Billy' Billingham, were in this Huey helicopter and I really wanted to beat him down, because I was SBS and he was SAS, and that rivalry dies hard. However, the helicopter pilot was quite inexperienced and, a bigger problem, the ropes were wet. So when I dropped out of the helicopter, I might as well have not had a rope: I went screeching downwards from 60 feet up and literally bounced off the floor. The recruits were all watching and saying, 'Fuck, how fast was that? Amazing!' But I injured myself big time – my leg was strapped up and I could hardly walk – and was off filming for three days.

Other times during filming, danger finds us. During series four in Chile, me and the lads were wandering around this reservoir, doing a locations recce, when we heard this big crack, like a single sniper round. Me and my fellow DS Ant Middleton turned around to see this big piece of rock hurtling towards us, spinning so fast it sounded like the whop-whop-whop of a helicopter's rotors. Luckily, it flew straight between us. Had it hit us, it would have taken our heads off. I guess that was some kind of message: you'd better make the most of life, because just around the corner there might be a piece of flying rock with your name on it.

In Morocco, the recruits were chucked from a helicopter and into some water, and I was assigned to keep an eye on those who weren't strong swimmers. When I popped up, I saw one of the recruits struggling and starting to panic. When I reached him, I shouted at him to relax and he grabbed hold of me and pulled me under. He was inadvertently drowning me in order to save himself! In the end, I had to punch him in the stomach to make him let go. The safety boat fished this guy out and when I reached the shore, Foxy was there to meet me. I said to him, 'Mate, he almost fucking killed me!' And in a quiet voice, so the microphone couldn't pick it up, Foxy said, 'Don't worry, dude, that will make for great TV...' I later discovered that the recruit had mistaken my 'just relax' for 'get on my back'. When in a state of panic, you'll hear whatever you want if it means you might survive.

Dan Cross was another amazing recruit from series three. He was away on business when he got a call from his wife, saying there was someone sniffing around the house. The next thing he knew, this guy was in the house and Dan was listening to his wife being stabbed to death, while she tried to protect their children. I'd been in warzones and lost friends, but that's what I signed up for. People dying is just part and parcel of being a soldier. But Dan's wife and children were entirely innocent, they hadn't signed up for anything.

I don't know how Dan found the strength to get through the trauma and not seek revenge. His kids are probably the only reason he's still here, otherwise he probably would have taken his own life. You'd expect someone like that to be broken 24 hours a day, seven days a week. But Dan has found a way to get on with his life and is getting remarried, which is just fantastic for him.

The story of Mark Peart, who appeared in series four, also hit me hard. Just months before we started filming, Mark arrived home to find his wife had taken her own life. Physically, he was the strongest on the course. But it was obvious that Mark still had a lot to deal with mentally. I just felt so much empathy for him, this bloke who had been left to pick up the pieces. Mark was one of only three recruits standing at the end, so at least he'd been able to channel all that negative injury into something positive.

Efrem Brynin was a recruit in series two, which took place in the jungle in Ecuador. Efrem was well into his forties and Ant actually said to him, 'You shouldn't be here, you should have your feet up in front of the fire.' But during one of our chats, he revealed that he was there because he lost his son in Afghanistan. Efrem was suffering a lot and I felt for him. Appearing on the show was the only way he felt he could get close to his son, maintain the connection, even though he was dead. That was a significant moment for me, because it made me view things from the outside looking in.

When you're in a warzone, you don't think about how it affects people back home. I didn't anyway. I cut myself off, because I thought connecting to any emotion at home would soften me and make me question why I was there. A warzone is a harsh environment and if you don't stay sharp, you're more likely to lose your life. As cruel as it might sound, the last thing you want to be doing is phoning home all the time and discovering that your loved ones are suffering. Or it might be something as innocuous as your son having the flu, the car breaking down, your wife's plans to redecorate the bathroom or your dog dying. Before you know it, your mind is at home, where it shouldn't be.

It relates to the idea of peace in war. A soldier will be sitting on the frontline with his mates, dealing with sporadic bits of danger, but their loved ones will be listening to stories on the radio and TV about bombs going off here, there and everywhere. They'll be reading about casualties in the newspaper and seeing pictures of carnage and maimed and dead bodies on the news. And their minds will be in turmoil, thinking about what might have become of their husband, son, father or brother. Efrem made me reflect on my family and what they'd been through, while I was busy not thinking about them.

My mum recently reminded me of some of the letters I sent her while I was serving in Iraq. In one of them, I describe watching over one of Saddam Hussein's palaces, before telling her we'd just shot two of Saddam's guards. I made it sound so blasé, as if it was the most normal thing in the world. And it must have shocked my mum, especially given that I was still so young. In the next sentence, I was asking her to send me some Wash & Go shampoo, some baby lotion – God knows what I wanted that for! – and some chocolates. Those letters summed up military life: most of it is very mundane, but suddenly you can be in a gunfight and dicing with death.

There was another letter that mum tells me made her cry. It read, 'Mum, do you remember me? I am your son Matthew. I've written so many letters to you and you haven't replied. I don't know if you realise what it's like out here. Please, please, please write to me.' She had been replying, but her letters had been held up in Tunisia. So in the next letter I wrote: 'Really sorry. Can you forgive me? What a shit bastard I've been.'

In the first series of *SAS: Who Dares Wins*, we gave the recruits the choice of phoning home or not. There weren't many people left and those who remained were physically and mentally exhausted. We advertised the phone call as a reward for all their efforts. But it was another trick, a test of resolve. Anyone with the right amount of focus shouldn't have made that phone call. For some people, hearing the voice of their girlfriend, mum or daughter was too much to bear. They came out of the room in tears. They were mentally and physically diminished and their determination was blunted. Suddenly they were riddled with self-doubt and asking themselves, 'Why am I here?' When asked why he declined to make a call, Ryan Roddy replied, 'Because I was scared it would cause me to lose focus.' That was a good answer.

In subsequent series, the recruits had to make a video call. Some came out of the room looking like they'd been hollowed out. Others emerged re-energised, determined to make it to the end for their loved ones. In series three, Jonny Davis closed his eyes all the way through his call. As well as being hard as nails, Jonny was very emotionally detached, much like Ryan. It didn't surprise me that Jonny was one of the last two men standing and to this day is a personal friend and training partner.

In series four in Chile, we had to sit and listen to one traumatic story after another. It exhausted me mentally. Every time I walked into that Mirror Room I thought, 'What's it going to be this time?'

At the same time, the DS's reaction to the stories is such an important part of the programme, because it humanises the Special Forces. When I was a kid, I thought Special Forces soldiers were superheroes, created on another planet and flown in on a spaceship, or cut from quarries. And people still say to me, 'You guys are cut from a different cloth.' We're not!

As I hope the programme shows, we're just normal blokes who happen to have done extraordinary things. We have a greater understanding of our own limitations than most people. We understand that boundaries are things we create ourselves, that they're not imposed by some outside force. But we're not these invulnerable alpha males or hard-nosed killers with no feelings.

We are aware of our emotions, but we know how to control them and use them to our advantage in conflict. That's not to say we don't struggle with our emotions in everyday life. I've been at the top of my game in the Special Forces to rock bottom in civilian life. I haven't had it any worse than anyone else but, all the same, I've been in some bad places. It's the same with the other lads on the show: Foxy, Ant and Billy. That makes us relatable and I hope it inspires people to do things they didn't think they were capable of.

Foxy went on national TV to talk about his PTSD, which was a brave and brilliant thing to do. The Special Forces turned their back on Foxy and asked him to leave, instead of offering to help, so him discussing his problems highlighted the lack of emotional support for veterans. Plus, there would have been people sitting at home, whose husbands, sons, fathers or brothers had served in war zones, thinking, 'Oh shit, if this bloke who served in the Special Forces is struggling, then maybe my husband/son/father/brother is feeling the same.'

Soldiers have been struggling with various forms of trauma since the beginning of time. The guys who fought in the First and Second World Wars suffered terribly after coming home, but their emotions were often locked away. It's bizarre that there were millions of men sitting in living rooms and pubs all over the country, not talking about the awful things they'd experienced. You'd often hear those old soldiers described as quiet men. My grandfather was like that, you didn't hear a lot from him. It was seen as noble and dignified not to talk about their problems. Men had to show a strong front, pretend they weren't affected by what they'd been through. But I look back now and realise there must have been so much going on inside my grandfather's head.

Until recently, soldiers felt embarrassed to share their problems, because they thought it was only them who was affected. When you think you're the only one, you become very alienated and insular. You lose your friends, because you don't think they'll understand. But one reason that soldiers are opening up now is because people have started to talk about their problems in public. People like Foxy. But there will still be plenty of soldiers out there, living with their secret struggles and not coping at all well. Another one of them was my old mate Goldie, a giant of a lad from South Africa – both physically and personality-wise – who was the daddy of 576 Troop during my Marines training. Goldie took his own life in 2017, which hit me hard. Goldie had lost his way and I was trying to find him work. But I had no idea how much he was suffering, and I wish I could have done more.

During my time in the military and on the circuit, there was nobody to speak to, no outlet for any negative thoughts. Even if there had been anybody to speak to, I don't think I would have taken the opportunity. When my mum came to Australia and I was in a bit of a mess, she could see that I was having problems, but I didn't want to go into them in any kind of detail.

Until fairly recently, a common view was that if a soldier was showing signs of mental illness, he was weak. A soldier is a pawn, and a soldier who doesn't put on a brave face and admits to having problems can be swept from the board, just like what happened to Foxy. No one wants to put their hand up and say they're weak. So I was programmed not to admit to anything, or even feel the need to. And if anyone else did, I'm sorry to say they had the piss taken out of them and it was turned into a joke. But if you don't share your problems, all those traumatic experiences build up in your brain. And the brain is like a pressure cooker, so that eventually the trauma starts leaking. It makes so much more sense to release that pressure of your own accord.

PTSD is not the preserve of the military. Someone can suffer PTSD after being raped, getting knocked over by a car, almost drowning, or a million and one other occurrences. I know that I suffered trauma as a child, because I can't really remember much other than the trauma. Not only was I attacked by a chimpanzee, hospitalised with gangrene, run over twice, in trouble with the law and sent to a remand home, I had a difficult relationship with my father. Taken as individual episodes, they might not sound like much. But individual episodes pile up until they're touching the ceiling and ready to break through.

But it's my belief that the term PTSD has become too generalised. Of course it exists, but it is quite specific. A lot of the suffering that veterans go through is caused by the loss of brotherhood. A soldier suddenly without his mates is like an animal suddenly separated from its pack. You take that camaraderie for granted, which breeds complacency. You no longer have that support network, you're weakened and vulnerable. One minute you were a fighting machine and suddenly you're not, and you don't even know why you're getting out of bed in the morning. That's when the problems start.

Unless you find a new purpose quickly, you start spiralling downwards. A lot of soldiers think that the grass will be greener on the other side and that they'll be fighting employers off in Civvy Street. But just because you were part of one of the finest fighting forces in the world doesn't mean people in civilian life will realise what you have to offer. Discipline and loyalty are massive assets, but so many companies fail to see it, while the veterans themselves seem to take those qualities for granted and think they're nothing special. To compound the problem, many soldiers lack confidence. They're not used to talking about their abilities, because in the military, they're not going to get a reaction. They're too humble for their own good. Some sit back and think, 'Surely someone will recognise what I've got to offer eventually.' They wait and wait and wait and their phone never rings. Lack of confidence and complacency are a destructive marriage.

People, including potential employers, don't care that they served their country. They don't even know where or why our military are serving. And it's very difficult to explain to people who have no basic understanding. That's one of the reasons I didn't want anyone to know I was in the military. I couldn't be doing with the small talk and stupid questions. Other people who do have a basic understanding think you've got a screw loose for wanting to be a soldier. So veterans end up thinking their service was pointless. Before they know it, they start to lose belief. And eventually, they feel entirely worthless.

That's why a lot of veterans end up on the street. They get depressed and self-medicate by hitting the drink and drugs. It's the transition itself that's traumatic, not necessarily anything you experienced while serving. Many soldiers return from military life with nothing more than a few dents in their armour. But soon that armour is rusting away and falling to pieces.

20

IRON LADIES

n 2018, the British Government announced that all roles in the military would be open to women, including those in the Special Forces. My immediate thought when I heard this was, 'If the UK Special Forces are so good at what they do, why would they risk changing that dynamic?'

The government's decision was obviously based on basic principles of gender equality. Quite rightly, if a woman wants to do a certain job, and demonstrates that she has the necessary attributes to do that job, then she should be allowed to do it. But I think the subject of women doing frontline soldiering is thornier than that. Fighting a war isn't really a job, it's a matter of life and death. And a warzone doesn't take societal norms into consideration.

If people assume that a mixed male and female Special Forces team is going to work the same as an all-male team, they're delusional. I don't subscribe to the view that men and women are the same, just as I don't see any problems in men and women being different. When a woman walks into a room full of men, it changes the group dynamic. I'm sure there are people out there who will say, 'If that's the case, then the men need to modify their behaviour.' Well, at least as it stands, people aren't selected for the Special Forces based on their political correctness and progressive views on gender equality, they're selected because they're the toughest soldiers in the country.

Men behave differently when women are around. Call me old-fashioned, but I'm quite gentlemanly around women. That's what society demanded I should be, or at least used to. I open doors and stand up on trains when a woman gets on and there's no seat. When I was growing up, that was just being respectful. And it's natural for men to be more protective of the opposite sex. That's the result of thousands of years of social programming. I'm not sure that's suddenly going to change if you have women fighting on the frontline. And if the changing of that dynamic affects people's ability to operate properly, that might mean people being killed who otherwise wouldn't be.

There are a lot of small details that I don't think have been considered. A lot of decompression involves hanging out with the lads in your dorm. Would women have to have separate sleeping quarters, with their own toilet facility? Has anyone considered how mixed teams might affect relationships? One minute you're off on a six-month tour with Gary and Trev, the next you're off on a six-month tour with Cindy and Kate. Military relationships are strained enough without girlfriends and wives worrying if their partners are having an affair with a workmate. And while relationships in the workplace are common nowadays, relationships on a frontline would be a different kettle of fish.

In series four of *SAS: Who Dares Wins*, we decided to pose the question: do women have the minerals to be considered for Special Forces Selection? We had an equal mix of men and women, and I'll happily admit the female recruits surprised me. Some of them were stronger, mentally and physically, than some of the men. And it was a question a lot of the public clearly wanted to see the answer to, because the ratings went through the roof.

I imagine there were a lot of men tuning in to see the women fall flat on their faces. But I hope there were a lot more men and women tuning in to see them defy expectations. The experiment proved to any boys and men watching at home that there are women out there who are infinitely tougher than them and have what it takes to do a job in the military. That's a positive message. Channel 4 desperately wanted a woman to be victorious, and that's how it turned out, with Lou McCullough one of only three recruits to make it to the end. But while I now know that there are women out there capable of getting on the start line of Special Forces Selection, I still have misgivings concerning the group dynamics.

At the end of the series, two of the recruits were seeing each other. Imagine that happening for real in a combat zone: you're running into contact, you've got Cindy to your right, Trev to your left and both go down. If you're in a relationship with Cindy, you're not going to think rationally. You're going to try to save her, regardless of whether that's the correct decision. In war, you shouldn't have to juggle with theoretical questions concerning what is or isn't politically correct, not when you're dealing with bombs, bullets and carnage.

On *SAS: Who Dares Wins*, we often ask the recruits who the weakest member of the group is. We need to know who's being rejected, because we can't see everything. Some people say they can't do it, but they have to. It's about being able to subdue your emotions and not let them get in the way of the facts. Your friend might be a great drinking buddy and buy you nice birthday presents, but they might be shit at their job. So you have to be able to push friendships to the side, because that person you hate might be better for the collective. In a warzone, that person you hate might save your life. If you throw women into the mix in a warzone, there won't just be friendships, there will be romantic relationships. And that's when things might end up skewed.

So it's not as easy as saying, 'Yeah, let's just do it.' It needs to be well received at the other end. And the reason I don't think it would be universally popular with male soldiers is because while they're trying to integrate women, lives could be at risk. That's not an argument some people want to hear, but I couldn't care less. If equality of opportunity has an adverse effect on quality of outcome, then you have a problem. Any changes that are made to an organisation have to improve things, otherwise you're just playing politics. The key question is, would the integration of women make the Special Forces a more effective fighting force? To be perfectly honest, I don't think it would. I'm not saying all-female teams wouldn't work, but until the day that there are enough women to create all-female teams, I'm not sure it's viable.

I think wanting to get one over the men gave the women an extra boost, but I also think the men were spurred on by not wanting to be beaten by a woman. You could see the frustration and annoyance in male recruits' faces when they dropped out while there were women remaining. That goes right back to the playground, when being beaten by a girl at anything physical is considered a joke. As pathetic as it is, that attitude stays with a lot of males into adulthood. But that competition between the sexes also produced negative results. Because the women were desperate to prove the men wrong, and the men were terrified of losing face, people were scared of showing any weaknesses and egos were inflated. And as I've already explained, inflated egos are a problem in the Special Forces.

There was also the notorious boxing match between a man and a woman, which caused a bit of a stir in the press. When recruit Louise picked fellow recruit Nathaniel out for a fight, Ant told Nathaniel not to hold back. And he didn't, leaving Louise bloodied and bruised. Predictably, some of the tabloids feigned horror, with headlines including: 'Female Contestant Brutally Battered By Male Rival'. But you can't have it both ways. You can't be for equality in the military while wanting women to be given special treatment. That would be patronising to women and drive down standards.

Ironically, Louise didn't seem to mind at all, while Nathaniel hated the fact he'd beaten her up. But equality of treatment would be thornier in reality. Can you imagine three men stripping a woman naked during Selection interrogation, as happened to me? Would anyone seriously do that? But that's exactly what they should do, because if a woman got captured behind enemy lines, there is a chance her captors would do more than just strip her.

Similarly, everyone carried the same weight, but you can tell yourself you're going to treat them all the same until you're blue in the face, the reality is rather different. For someone like me, who idolises his mother, it's very difficult to give a woman a proper bollocking, point out their deficiencies and call them horrible names. It's just not in my nature. During the series, I was also more inclined to encourage the women. There was a recruit called Nadine, who I stuck with for a day, giving her as much encouragement as possible. I didn't mean to patronise her, that was me simply being nicer to a woman than I would be to a man. People will no doubt say, 'That's your problem, not theirs.' But that's just how a lot of men are wired, and if you translate that into a Special Forces situation, that's not a good dynamic.

In a way, the DS on the show are a surrogate enemy, just the same as they are in Special Forces Selection. I watch the show back and sometimes think, 'Jesus, I didn't realise I was that nasty.' But the other lads call me Corporal Cuddles, because they think I'm too compassionate and quick to praise them – especially Billy, who scares the recruits shitless.

I found the chats with women in the Mirror Room particularly difficult. When Nadine told us that she'd been sexually assaulted and had a terrible time with men in general, I didn't know what to do. When a woman starts crying, my natural reaction is to put my arm around them and tell them everything is going to be OK. But I would never do that with a male recruit. Once we got them all together, we could really cut loose. But when it was one-on-one with a woman, I found it very hard to do.

Once again, that's problematic, because it's not like we're horrible for no reason. Turning civilians into soldiers takes a series of short, sharp shocks because it's such a steep learning curve. That's why you have the stereotype of the bullying sergeant major, constantly shouting at his men. Imagine commanding a non-motivated team in war, conscripts who can't even function on Civvy Street. I can't even comprehend that, it's an almost impossible task. If you hammer them into shape fast, there's an outside chance they'll pick up their game and fight when the bullets start flying. But even if you do, it's far more likely that they'll freeze instead, which must have happened on many occasions.

Whether Lou, Milo or the other winner of series four, Mark Peart, have what it takes to do a job in the Special Forces is another matter entirely (although I'm sometimes asked which squadron the winners are now serving in!). I'd like to be able to say that anyone who is still standing at the end of the show has it in them to pass Selection. But all I can say with any certainty is that they show the necessary qualities. To pass Selection, you must have a military career in the first place. And you can fail Selection on so many different things. You might get injured, you might have problems at home, you might even be accused of punching a farmer. The Selection process is far more long-winded and complicated than *SAS: Who Dares Wins*, and a lot more can go wrong in seven months than eight days.

But while I have no doubt that there are women in the UK who are physically and mentally capable of passing Selection, I'm not sure there are many women out there thinking, 'I want a piece of the action in Special Forces.' People only think about the glory and the glamour and the patriotism. But the reality of Special Forces is hiding in an observation post, watching a target for days on end and shitting in a zip-lock bag in front of your mates. It's travelling to a foreign land, not seeing your friends and family for months on end and killing strangers. It's seeing your mates get shot and blown up.

That's why I'm not a fan of some of the new military adverts, which make life on the frontline seem rather cosy: there are people making each other cups of tea, people praying on their mat in the middle of combat. Don't get me wrong, soldiers are nice to each other. But the adverts don't mention that you might see mutilated bodies hanging from trees. It's false advertising, almost tricking people. Next thing you know, they'll bring out an advert that shows soldiers breaking off from a fire fight to have a group hug. If only that was the case. But the truth is, war really isn't much to write home about.

* * *

SAS: Who Dares Wins entered more uncharted territory when we invited celebrities to have a taste of Special Forces Selection. When we got them off the boat, they still had their hoods on. But even when they took their hoods off, I didn't know who any of them were. That's more a reflection of me than their level of fame, because I don't really watch TV or follow sport. I said to Foxy, 'Who the fuck are these people?' Luckily, Foxy does watch a bit of TV and loves his sport. And I had to do plenty of research on them.

I thought the celebrity version would be a bit fluffy. I worried about their motivation, because they were already famous. And I suspected that as soon as they hit a bit of hardship, they'd chuck in the towel. Obviously, it wasn't difficult to find out about their past online, and there were plenty of tears in the Mirror Room. And interrogation cracked a few of them. But some of them stuck it out, and I really respected them for that, because they didn't have to.

A few celebrities stood out. Camilla Thurlow was famous for her massive social media following and finishing second on *Love Island* a couple of years ago. In short, she's not the kind of person you'd expect to do well on *SAS: Who Dares Wins*. But she defied expectations. I shouldn't have been that surprised. Camilla is a former humanitarian worker who has actually done a lot of good with her celebrity, including making a documentary highlighting the plight of landmine victims in Cambodia. And a lot of celebrities possess one of the key Special Forces ingredients: resilience. Because you have to be resilient to stay relevant and deal with being in the public eye.

When Victoria Pendleton's name came up and I started researching her, I wondered if we were doing the right thing having her on the show. I even received emails, telling me to treat her carefully. Victoria had a great career as a track cyclist, winning untold medals, but had spoken openly about her struggles with mental illness, even telling the press that she'd planned to take her own life after a recent marriage split and a failed attempt to climb Everest. Victoria had a lot to prove, and I was worried that if it went badly for her on the show, it might send her spiralling back into depression. But she did really well and I hope she got a boost from it, just as I hope everyone who appears on the show does.

But the star of the show for me was former Chelsea and England footballer Wayne Bridge. Footballers aren't really known for their toughness, with good reason. You'll see them get a nudge in the back and they'll be rolling about on the floor as if they've been shot. But Wayne was an absolute legend and hard as nails.

Because we didn't want to treat the celebrities (although as sportspeople Wayne and Victoria aren't strictly celebrities) any different from our normal candidates, we spoke to Wayne in depth about his former girlfriend's alleged affair with ex-Chelsea teammate and England captain John Terry, which opened a few old wounds. But there was more to Wayne's story than that. He's very frustrated, because he doesn't know what to do with his life. He had a great football career, won the Premier League, the FA Cup and played in a World Cup. But he's still only in his thirties. He's got plenty of money, a beautiful wife and kids, but is struggling to find a purpose. His situation is not dissimilar to military veterans, shorn of the buzz and the brotherhood. I really hope that his showing in *SAS: Who Dares Wins* proves to be a defining break point.

21

THE BUSINESS

As soon as I signed the contract for *SAS: Who Dares Wins*, I knew the business would follow. It dovetailed perfectly, we started getting traction from day one. I bought domain names, got busy marketing and Break-Point's first course took place while the first series of the show was being broadcast. It had been a very slow process, there had been a lot of doubts and every penny I earned from the show had gone into the business. But it was finally happening.

When Laura walked into my life, it was further proof that the stars had finally aligned. I met her while we were both working for the hostile environment training company. And although I wasn't actively looking for a new partner, it soon became obvious that we shared almost identical visions. At the time, Laura was seeing another guy from our team. But one night, we were all having a few drinks in the pub when she asked about a tattoo on my forearm. When I told her it represented the children we'd saved in Thailand, me and her were pretty much a done deal. Her bloke went to the bar to get the drinks in and by the time he got back, him and Laura were pretty much history.

I wasn't everyone's idea of an ideal catch when we met. When some work came up in London, I had nowhere to stay, so ended up living in a tent. One of Laura's friends put me up at the bottom of their garden. To be fair, I couldn't stay in the house, because it was full up with kids. And they probably thought, 'He's SAS, he'll love it out there!' And while it wasn't where I expected to be living in my mid-forties, it was nice and peaceful and meant I was able to continue with my planning and visualisation. And when Laura managed to get a council flat, it was there that Break-Point finally came to fruition.

Laura had been in the training world for a long time and loved the idea of Break-Point. She shared my passion and vision and was everything I'd ever wanted in a girlfriend. She has such a beautiful way about her and I struggle to pick a fault with her. She's almost flawless, like an angel that has been sent specifically for me.

After we met, I gave up drinking. Laura didn't really drink much anyway, but when she realised I wanted to stop, she said she'd do it with me. That was a drastic departure from anyone else I'd ever been out with. And who knows, if I hadn't met Laura when I did, I might have met yet another boozer and it would have been mayhem all over again.

Giving up the booze was such a huge thing for me, although it wasn't easy, because I'd been waging a mental battle with it for such a long time. I knew alcohol wasn't for me, but I kept on drinking it anyway. That led to self-loathing, which manifested itself as anger. I'd tell myself I'd quit for a month, but after a week the battle would be on again. I just couldn't understand what I should have been doing instead. And it was only really during filming for series two of SAS: *Who Dares Wins* that I finally managed to get on top of it. When the eight weeks of filming were up, I'd found so much clarity and focus. And I thought, 'This is amazing. Why would I want to stop feeling like this? Why would I want to corrupt the chemistry?' My mum tells me that since I stopped drinking, I'm a completely different person. I'm her son again – the soppy boy who loves a hug and a kiss – not that angry, disconnected person who was masquerading as him.

Not drinking made it so much easier to visualise the business. Your brain is like a farm. It can get overgrown and you have to keep weeding it and planting good thoughts. But as soon as you hit the bottle, it's like a hurricane howling through, tearing everything up before you've even had the chance to harvest. I've got a short amount of time to push Break-Point globally, and if I looked back in five years' time and thought, 'I made mistakes because I was too busy on the piss', I'd be in a world of hurt. I blew all the money I made in Iraq on booze, houses and failed relationships. But now was the chance to get as much traction for Break-Point as possible, so that when *SAS: Who Dares Wins* comes to an end, the business will have the momentum to keep going for a long, long time.

From being a soldier who conformed to the drinking culture in the military, I've now gone to the other extreme. Everything is extremes with me, nothing is middle of the road. I try not to judge people, but whereas I used to say to people, 'Why the fuck are you not drinking?', I'll now find myself thinking the complete opposite. I did get a bit holier than thou in those early stages, to the extent that I wouldn't go to the pub with my mum and her husband Simon when I visited them in Cornwall. But now I'm happy to go along and even have the odd beer.

I honestly think I've got some kind of PTSD from drinking, because when I have a beer in my hand, I start getting flashbacks to all the trauma it caused me. Drinking messes with my head and makes me spiral out of control. I tried to have a drink at a function recently and couldn't even force it down me. It irritated me, because I'd spent so much money on alcohol in the past and now it was only when I was getting it for free that I realised it was pointless.

If I'd been with Laura when I was in the Special Forces, I probably would have stayed in, because she would have supported everything I did. She would have gone through all the hardships without moaning and making me feel bad. All the time I was away, she was the person I was wishing for, even if only subconsciously: somebody who is spiritual and interested in the development of the mind. She's got a little boy called William to raise but has made so many sacrifices for the sake of me and Break-Point.

Laura is creative and has loads of ideas, some of them nuts, most of them great. When I get stressed about the business, she calms me down. She often puts me first, but not all the time. That's crucial: when you're on a plane and things go wrong, you have to put on your own gas mask before you can assist anyone else.

I sometimes ask myself, 'If I hadn't met Laura, would I have achieved what I have with Break-Point?' It's a difficult question to answer, but also irrelevant: it's been great doing it with her, which is all that matters. Laura has been there every step of the way, and I'll always be there to support her. That's how any relationship should be.

* * *

On the first Break-Point course, Foxy and I wanted people to experience exactly what took place on the show. I'd bought a load of gear from the programme makers – Bergens, fatigues, boots, the lot, including a load of shit I didn't end up using – sold 15–20 tickets, but had no real clue what we were doing. We were throwing more and more kit at it, which was costing us more than we were bringing in. It was all about survival, which, luckily, I'm quite good at.

I'd pulled in staff I used to work with from hostile environment training, because we thought we'd have to give people quite a hard time to teach them the skills. But because some people were there as fans of *SAS: Who Dares Wins,* we had to compromise a little. We were seeing pictures of girls with orange tans and long fingernails on the medical forms. People were turning up with pyjamas and hair straighteners. We had a girl called Michelle working for us at the time, and she was ex-army and like a little terrier. I left her and Laura in charge of the processing tent, where people had all their home comforts taken from them on arrival. And when I walked in, there were bottles of make-up and nail varnish remover on the table.

I said to Michelle, 'What the hell are you doing?'

'We're stripping them down to their bare bones.'

'Stop! People are paying for this, you've got to let them enjoy it!'

We were overstaffed and disorganised, but that first course was brilliant. Most of the people who turned up were the type who lived in a box, travelled to work in a box, worked in a box, went home in a box and repeated the same journey from box to box to box every day. So just staying out overnight and eating army rations was an eye-opener for them.

I think the fact that we were real-life Special Forces veterans helped. They soon realised that we weren't just killing machines behind masks, we were people who genuinely cared about them and their development. Not only that, we believed that the stuff we learned in the Special Forces, and life, also applied to them.

There was one guy on that first course who clearly demonstrated the difference the company was going to make. He was virtually homeless, living in his car, but had scraped together enough money from a carpentry job to pay for the course. A year later, he sent us a message saying how that course had saved his life. He'd got himself a full-time job, a house and started exercising again. I had no real idea the business was going to touch people so deeply, but we're now inundated with similar stories of transformation and positive growth.

* * *

We were soon inundated with emails from people asking for help. One girl, who had done 18 years in the military, emailed to say that she was suffering from PTSD and thinking of killing herself. She had the rope ready. She needed help and the conventional methods weren't working for her. A lot of help that charities provide is process driven, involving filling out forms and assessments, and people with PTSD can't face doing things like that.

I replied to the girl, saying that I would try to help and please not to do anything rash. Break-Point is a business that needs to make money. We can help people with PTSD and other forms of mental illness, but we're not a charity. But we've had strong relationships with charities from the start, so can refer people on. So I put the girl in touch with Rock2Recovery, which was co-founded by Foxy and provides help to serving soldiers and veterans suffering with mental illness. Rock2Recovery didn't have any long-winded processes, so they could start trying to deal with the girl's problems immediately. That girl now says that without that happening, she wouldn't be here anymore.

Break-Point does a lot of stuff on facing fears, whether of confined spaces or heights. We put people in challenging scenarios and help them through. Breathing is a major factor, because it provides clarity and prevents people from being overwhelmed by the situation. We built a 40-foot tower for people to abseil off, and to see the girl in question on top of that tower, talking people down, was incredible. Afterwards, people were telling me how amazing she was. This was a girl who came close to hanging herself, who found it too stressful to drive or even catch a train, and now she was driving from Birmingham to Sussex and providing emotional support to others. Seeing things like that convinced me that Break-Point was making a difference.

Break-Point's mission statement is: to create a globally identifiable brand recognised for the positive growth and development of others. As such, since those early days, the courses have tended to be less physical and more focused on mindset, how we work as humans and personal growth. We've had to create a horrible course, called DENIED, which is as close to Special Forces Selection as we could design – ethically and legally – because there are people out there who want to be thrashed beyond belief. But that's not really what corporate groups are after. Some request to be tested physically, but essentially they want to have fun, while learning transferable skills from the world of Special Forces that will be of value to them in their work and everyday life.

On our courses, I talk about the survival blueprint, which is the tendency to look for things to go wrong, which in turn leads to people living in the repeat cycle of yesterday I've already mentioned. That's how humans have evolved, because so much could go wrong when we were living as hunter-gatherers. Everyone struggles with mindset, and if you don't find out how your mind works, you'll constantly think there's something wrong with you. If you do find out how your mind works, things that were previously stressful become easier to deal with.

At Break-Point, we work with companies from the corporate world. And whatever the industry, the people are a company's roots. That's why we concentrate on the individual, how they can improve themselves, and therefore the company they work for. Never mind piling loads of training on your employees, you have to start at the bottom, which means developing them as people. If a company neglects its workforce, it will wither and die.

So many workers in the corporate world don't even know what their company's mission statement is. I couldn't get my head around that. How can you not know why you're getting out of bed every morning and going to work? So, at the team and leadership level, we put a lot of work into creating mission statements. If the company already has an overarching mission statement that is vague or meaningless, individual departments and branches should create new ones, tangible goals that can be broken down into milestones. If you don't have that in place, your office will be like a grown-up crèche. Our clients that have adopted this have witnessed amazing growth.

Mission Success Cycles are a military thing and there are hundreds of them. One of the basics is SMEAC: Situation, Mission, Execution, Administration/Logistics, Command/Signal. But all Mission Success Cycles boil down to: Plan, Brief, Deliver, Debrief. In military and business environments, processes deliver results, not emotions. But processes don't happen in a lot of offices.

While I was working for the oil and gas company in Australia, I didn't have one team meeting in two years. Employees hadn't been set any objectives. If you don't have objectives, you don't have a purpose. And employees without a purpose are just working the payroll. Money should be a by-product, but if it becomes the focus, your company will under-achieve. I just couldn't understand a billion-dollar company not investing in its workforce. It was a massive organisation but the whole team ethic had got lost somewhere along the way.

Employees had no idea what good or bad work looked like, because there were no debriefs. The leadership debriefs we have on *SAS: Who Dares Wins* mirror what takes place in Special Forces Selection. They're called 'prayer meetings', apparently because during the Aden Emergency in the 1960s, the only time the SAS could get together for a debrief was while the locals were praying, including the bad guys. Prayer meetings are about reflecting on the day's work and pooling opinions. During Selection, that information isn't fed back to the soldiers, they'll just be shown a red card if they're not performing. But in a corporate environment, that information should be discussed with employees, so that improvements can be made.

You could have the best people in the world working for you, but if they're not motivated, goal-driven and focused, they won't do the job to the best of their ability and produce results. But people have come on our courses, come back and told us their company's culture has changed because of Break-Point. For that reason, they'll tell us it's the best training they've ever done.

A Special Forces team will consist of many different characters. There will be someone who's particularly driven, someone who's particularly analytical, someone who's particularly creative or someone who's particularly empathetic. So before they come on a course, we have the corporate employees do something called PRISM, which is an online assessment tool created by neuroscientist Colin Wallace, a former member of army Intelligence and psychological warfare expert. PRISM defines which kind of character you are, because unless you understand what kind of character you are, you'll struggle to develop.

When I did my first PRISM test and received my results, I thought they'd mixed me up with someone else. They said I was really creative with a good deal of empathy, which didn't ring true to me. I thought I was more of a driven type. But because the test asks questions in so many different ways, it prevents you from delivering your own perception of yourself. You're unable to trick it, there's no escaping the truth.

It's a bit scary suddenly discovering who you really are and that you spent years trying to be a person you weren't. What's even scarier is that I actually knew who I was – consider my love of music and clothes as a kid and my artistic streak – but had buried those inclinations. The fact that so many people never find out who they really are explains why they spend their lives doing the wrong things, and spending your life doing things that don't suit your true personality can lead to serious frustration, anger issues and mental illness.

The PRISM test results help us build project teams for corporates. You can't have a team that consists exclusively of people with the same characteristics, you need some of everything. And you don't make someone who's creative do hours and hours of analytical reports. A good manager will pick the right people for the right jobs, which requires a good understanding of each member of staff's strengths and weaknesses. Sometimes you won't have a choice, so you have to also be able to adapt. An ideal Special Forces team will consist of individuals with particular roles – a medic, a demolitions expert, this, that and the other – but who can do everything extremely competently.

One of the beauties of the Special Forces is that we're a group of leaders within a team, all sharing the same goal. The traditional view of leadership and hierarchy doesn't exist in the Special Forces. Everyone is encouraged to speak up, say what they think might be wrong or could be improved. Effective businesses will have a similar ethos, but it's a hard thing to change in the corporate world. And, to be fair, that hierarchical system also exists in the conventional army, for good reason. It's very easy to say, 'Let's flatten everything out and get rid of hierarchies', but you have to have a strong team to be able to implement that policy. If you can't be sure that your recruits are dependable, you have to crack the whip.

If you give a fuckwit responsibility and flexibility, before you know it he'll be running around doing a load of shit that's not constructive. You might also have to crack the whip if you're managing manual workers, because the environment they're working in is so demotivating and most of them won't feel anything for the company's mission.

You could, however, flatten out the hierarchy in a sports team, when there are only a few members and individual responsibility and flexibility are keys to success. It amazes me that we haven't had more sports teams approach our company, because they could learn a lot from the way the Special Forces do things. You often hear it said that great sports teams have an almost telepathic understanding, whether it be the All Blacks in rugby or Manchester City in football. Each player knows exactly where he is meant to be on the field at any given time, and also that his teammates will be where he expects them to be. That unthinking understanding, that sense of absolute trust, only comes from a very high degree of training. And, paradoxically, that very high degree of training means you take that unthinking understanding for granted.

That's how it is in the Special Forces, except for one key difference. On some missions, a team of four soldiers who barely knew each other might be thrown together in an instant, and they have to hit the ground running. They may never have worked with each other as a team, but there will be an understanding that they are the elite and that each one of them can be trusted.

While I enjoyed running as a kid, I was never interested in team sports. In fact, I was a bit of a loner. People assume that everyone in the Special Forces is a team player, but a Special Forces team would better be described as a group of loners who nevertheless understand the mechanics of teamwork. When I went on missions in the SBS, we didn't have to like each other, just as the best sports teams will contain players who don't like each other. There were blokes who had shagged other bloke's wives, people who hated each other with a passion outside of work. But when it came to doing the work, they were bang on it. Had that not been the case, people would have been killed. A company's mission statement can't take into account the fact that some of their staff don't like each other. But if you set clear objectives, that shouldn't really matter.

Generally speaking, the larger a company gets, the more a hierarchical system is needed, because the bosses know that not all of their staff will be up to the job and committed to the cause. But a common problem with hierarchies in large companies is that you end up with robotic promotion and managers becoming managers based on nothing apart from the fact that they've been there for a long time. That can leave a company with a layer of middle-managers who aren't particularly good at the job they used to do and a raft of staff below them who don't have any respect for their abilities.

A good team leader will be highly competent but also understand that someone within their team might be better than them at doing certain jobs. A bad team leader will think, 'I'm team leader, therefore I must know best about everything.' You can't possibly know better about everything than everyone else. A good team leader gives clear direction, motivates and allows other people to take glory for the wins. And a good team leader accommodates talented non-conformists, and people who prefer to operate outside the system, without complaint. There are limits, but if someone can do the job better than anyone else, why would you be bothered about the fact they turn up half an hour late or take an extra half an hour for lunch? But some leaders can't handle people bending the rules. They see it as a threat to their authority.

When I worked in an office environment, there were these martyrs who'd stay late every night and moan about it very publicly.

The bosses saw them as hard workers and worthy of promotion. But I'd think, 'These people just can't handle their workload or manage their time properly.' It was all about perception rather than actual value. It's not the hours you do, it's what you do in those hours. I'd rather have someone come in for five hours and work flat-out than come in for ten hours and be a passenger. Or if someone shows they can produce good work from home, don't come in at all.

A lot of companies spend all their time looking externally, at the competition. But you need to look inside first. Get that working correctly and the results will flow. If you don't get that working correctly, when the shit hits the fan, it will be very difficult to pull the team together and refocus. Sometimes people say to me, 'You worked in the Special Forces, where everyone was brilliant at their job, but I've got a load of fuckwits working for me.' And I tell them that it doesn't matter if you're an astronaut, banker or binman, we're all human. We all tend to make decisions based on emotion, and lessons from a Special Forces perspective carry extra weight, because we make our decisions while under a massive amount of pressure.

Given enough time, most people can be whipped into shape. But there are lost causes. There has to be a will, they've got to be motivated to change. And the people who come on Break-Point's courses are motivated, otherwise they wouldn't have signed up. They believe that life should be about continual improvement, day in, day out, even if you're already in a good place.

You've got to keep moving and keep progressing. Slowing down or stopping will mean you keep flopping around in that repeat cycle of yesterday, like an old jumper on a slow spin in a washing machine. But if you maintain momentum, you will eventually be thrown out of that cycle. You might have to cross some negative ground to reach your goal, but you will reach your goal eventually. And when that happens, your head will be a more pleasant place.

22

IN CONTROL

In *SAS: Who Dares Wins*, we orchestrate false endings all the time, to test the mental strength of the recruits. In series three, we ran them up a mountain and back down again, before pointing them in the direction of transport and telling them how well they'd all done. When we started doling out encouragement, anyone in their right mind knew something was up. Sure enough, just as they were about to jump into the transport, it started rolling away. And after the transport had disappeared over the horizon, the recruits were given an extra dose of beasting.

That kind of psychological messing will break a lot of people. As soon as they see the transport, they'll switch off mentally. And when they see it driving off into the distance, they'll abandon all hope. It's like reaching the top of a mountain and suddenly realising you've got to climb another one. It sounds like a cruel trick to play, but our DS had it done to us loads of times and it served a purpose. As a soldier, you don't get to choose when a battle stops. You have no idea when it's going to end, unlike a marathon or a rugby match. You might have already emptied yourself, you might be in absolute pieces, but if you get downhearted and lose momentum, that's dangerous.

The worst thing you can do in a warzone is stand still. The Special Forces are looking for people who stand up when things go wrong, not stand down; they're looking for people who increase their speed when they see the target, not lose enthusiasm; they're looking for people who don't just reach the target but push through it, while understanding that the end won't come when they want it to and the cycle might continue. This translates to everyday life. When you're standing at the top of whatever your metaphorical mountain might be, that's when you're at your most vulnerable. You've reached your goal, you're mentally drained and your defences are down, which is why so many people who achieve great success in life are quickly toppled from the peak.

My life has been full of false endings. Achieving my goals was always anti-climactic and it was never long before I was having to set a new one. From the age of 14, all I wanted to be was a soldier. But when I became a Royal Marine, it didn't make me happy. I thought joining the Special Forces would give me the purpose that I craved, but that didn't happen either. And I certainly didn't find meaning doing security in the madhouse that was Iraq.

* * *

I don't believe in regrets. It's a well-worn cliché, but it's the journey, however uncomfortable, that provides the growth. That's where the worthwhile stuff happens. Traumatic childhoods, failed relationships, disillusionment with work, all of that tough stuff provides lessons to learn from. That doesn't necessarily mean life gets easier, but it should get better.

I should reiterate that I'm lucky to have always had an extremely positive disposition. It was that disposition that enabled me to plough through everything that went awry in my childhood, join the Royal Marines and SBS, quickly recover from failed relationships and overcome any traumatic experiences while I was working in Iraq. It was the military that developed my ability to detach myself from bad situations. That ability to switch off and distance yourself, although it has its downsides, makes you more resilient in the face of adversity. In the Special Forces, you've got to be able to recover from knocks quickly. Shit happens, life is tough. As bleak as it sounds, it's entirely possible that more things will go wrong in your life than go right. But if you dwell on the negatives, you'll end up in a state of mental paralysis.

I'm sometimes asked whether I would have liked to have seen more action during my time in the military. After all, and as I've already made clear, that's what I signed up for. But when you've been shot at for real, you don't really want to be shot at again. I guess it's like asking an old punch-drunk boxer if he wishes he'd had more wars in the ring. Some would say yes, just as some soldiers tend to glorify the battles they were in. But soldiers who served in 'great' battles often end up with severe physical and mental issues, and I don't believe in short-term wins that don't establish long-term benefits.

For someone who initially yearned to experience war, now I see how terrible it all is. Like it or not, we have to have a military, because there will always be people out there who want to do us harm. But war certainly doesn't do its participants much good. I have old friends who have returned to civilian life saddled with problems. Some are missing limbs, but many of the injuries they carry are hidden. In contrast, I came through it relatively unscathed.

I've been strong enough to give up the booze, which causes so many problems among veterans, and set up five companies under the Break-Point brand. And I've finally discovered what makes me happy. In fact, it wasn't until I returned to the UK and got Break-Point up and running that I felt fulfilled and content for the first time in my life. I had a taste of it in Thailand, when I was attempting to save children from the sex trade, but even then I was away from the people I loved.

Between the ages of 18, when I joined the military, and 43, when I came home from Australia, I hardly saw Mum. Even now, she'll phone me after an episode of *SAS: Who Dares Wins* and say, 'Wow, that was amazing. I didn't know you could run down mountain faces and jump out of helicopters. Especially at the age of 48!' When you're away for as long as I was, the intimacy fades. It almost becomes more natural not to talk, and I don't want that to happen again. She deserves better for all that she's done. And so do I.

My relationship with Luke is great nowadays, although we don't do much yomping through the countryside or climbing mountains together, as I thought we might when he was born. I recently took him up the Pen y Fan, where I did the Hills Phase during Selection, and it was like he was going to die. The Wi-Fi connection isn't great up there, and a father depriving his son of Wi-Fi is tantamount to child abuse. To be fair, a lot of teenagers are like that. And I can hardly claim to be surprised that he hasn't inherited my love of the outdoors, because we've spent so much time apart. But we're getting closer.

It hasn't been a conventional father-and-son relationship by any means, just as my relationship with my father wasn't conventional. But after I left Luke, I saw my dad in a different light. He wasn't happy, so he decided to do something about it. That made no sense to me as a kid, but suddenly it did. His lack of financial support after he left was difficult to forgive and I'll never be as close to him as I am to my mum. But he's still my dad.

When you're a kid, you resent being made to do things you don't like. But your parents better understand the world they're preparing you for. You're not a kid forever, and I sometimes wonder if I'd have done the things I did if I'd been brought up soft. I certainly wouldn't have known how to saw the stock off a shotgun. And all those long walks with the dogs certainly gave me a love of the outdoors. As much as I resented Dad, I'm not sure I would have made it in the military if it wasn't for what he gave me. A psychiatrist would no doubt tell me that I was always trying to impress him, but never felt I lived up to his expectations. It caused me anguish, but it also put some grit into me. Like it or not, you are your father's son. I thank Dad for bringing me up with manners and teaching me the benefit of a hard day's work. I love him and I'll always be there for him.

Now that I've found my niche, which is changing people's lives through Break-Point, it's sometimes difficult to remember me as I was. That's partly because I didn't even know who I was. I bounced all over the world, was constantly trying to redefine myself. But now that I've discovered who I am and what I'm for, I'm more comfortable with my past.

* * *

For years, I tried to escape from the military and anything associated with it, but it just kept dragging me back in. And I'm proud to have been part of that big machine and to now be representing it on *SAS: Who Dares Wins*. Every time I open my mouth on that show, I think about my responsibilities as a veteran. It's important that I don't act like an idiot, because people tend to stereotype. If viewers think I am an idiot, they might think everyone in the Special Forces is an idiot, which couldn't be further from the truth.

I'm not interested in fame. I like being on TV because of the value I see in it, which is as promotion for my business and the charities I support, not because of anything it means to me. In 2018, I was incredibly proud to be made an official ambassador of The Royal Marines Charity. The marines opened their doors for me when I needed it, now it's my time to repay the debt, helping veterans and their families in whichever way I can. I recently launched a charity called StrongMen with Efrem and Dan from *SAS: Who Dares Wins*. StrongMen helps people who have developed mental health issues through bereavement, something that is close to both Efrem and Dan's hearts. Plans are afoot to raise money for StrongMen by climbing Mont Blanc, with Mark Peart, Milo Mackin and his brother Corbin. And I'm sure we'll have many more adventures beyond that.

I'm also looking at making a TV programme about troubled kids, which will endeavour to show them how lucky they actually are in relation to other kids around the world. The idea stemmed from my time in Thailand, where seeing kids who had been sold into prostitution put my own upbringing into sharp perspective.

I don't mind being recognised when I'm out and about, but I'm not sure how I'd cope with people constantly pointing at me and shouting, 'Look! It's that bloke from that SAS show!' I hate the city, almost everything about it winds me up. Fortunately, I live in the middle of nowhere.

I need to be isolated from the trivialities of everyday life. The more isolated the better. People frustrate me. I have no patience with small talk or petty gripes. Often, there will be nothing significant going on in someone's life, so they'll go hunting for problems. That raises their energy levels in the short term, but people get addicted to problems and end up stuck in a negative cycle. I look around at people on the Tube and they look so miserable. They remind me of zombies. They're on auto-pilot, going through the motions. And when they get home, they'll switch on the TV or stare at their phones, poisoning their minds with a relentless cycle of bad news, soap operas and panel shows. That's a lot of people's priorities, but I refuse to be sucked in. I don't watch the news, read newspapers or consume anything that will have a negative effect on my brain.

The above might make me sound like an old curmudgeon, but the fact that I seal myself off from any negativity means I'm not. Whereas now I might get irritated by someone's driving, before I would have been furious. I had anger inside me like you would not believe, but now I've found peace.

I've got so much passion for what I'm doing and the feeling I get from helping people is like the hit from a drug. For the first time in my life I'm working for myself, so have a feeling of control. People keep telling me about exit plans for the business, building something big and selling it. But I can't imagine ever wanting to. And I don't worry about becoming disillusioned, like I've become disillusioned with everything else, because I have finally found my calling. Having worked out who I am, the battle is over and I can finally flow.

I sometimes hear people opine that they haven't stumbled across their calling. But not many people do. You need to want to change. You need to set goals and visualise. That will smooth the path to a better future. Even when I was in my darkest places – addicted to booze and prescription drugs and thinking about ending it all – I managed to create a small window through which to clamber. When I felt that break point approaching, I breathed deeply and recalibrated. I calculated that things might have to get less comfortable before things got better. But the alternative was tapping out and rolling over.

There are long-term benefits in talking about the bad things that happened in your life, whatever horrors it conjures. I still get anxious when I tell the story of the chimp attack. When I close my eyes, I can see the chimp's face pressed against mine, her eyes ablaze, her teeth dripping with blood. But I also remember making that difficult decision to save my life. No one swooped down and saved me, it was my actions that changed my outcome for the better.

I had to be tough to serve in the Special Forces, but as you've discovered, I'm just a mummy's boy really. And even the toughest can be fragile. We all have our break points. But that doesn't mean we'll break. And you might even find a silver lining.

EPILOGUE

few years ago, I met up with my best Marines mate Troy Robson, for the first time in years. We grabbed a couple of beers, sat ourselves down and Troy said to me, 'Ollie, I've got a funny tale to tell you...'

Troy had been a colour sergeant for Alpha Company, 40 Commando, out in Camp Bastion, Afghanistan. Due to the activity of the enemy, many of the vehicles had been blown up, which had crippled his company's operational capability. So Troy kept sending emails to the relevant people and kept getting the same response: 'Nobody is getting vehicles because we don't have any.' But Troy doesn't take no for an answer.

He somehow managed to get access to the military transport officer's office, walked in and said, 'Sir, it's Sergeant Robson, I've been sending you emails about vehicles for my lads.'

'What the fuck are you doing in here? Get out, otherwise I'll have you arrested.'

'But sir, I need vehicles—'

'Get out!'

'But sir, we can't conduct operations without them—'

'Robson, this is your last chance to leave of your own accord.'

But just before Troy opened the door, the officer said to him, 'Before you go, Sergeant Robson, do you know Ollie Ollerton?'

Troy stopped in his tracks and swivelled on his heels.

'Do I know fucking Ollie? I joined up with him, back in 1989! We served in Northern Ireland and Iraq together, but when he joined the Special Forces, we lost contact. Why do you ask?'

'I've been looking for that boy for most of my career.'

'Really? Why's that, sir?'

'I was with him when he was attacked by the chimpanzee.'

The officer was Major James Stafford, who was with me at the circus that day and ran home – very quickly, for a chubby lad – to tell my mum about the attack. Major Stafford had probably asked every Marine he'd ever met if they knew me. It was like another weird scene from *Apocalypse Now*.

After Troy had recovered from the shock of stumbling across a first-hand witness to his old mate's chimp attack, while scrounging for vehicles in a warzone, he took a seat. Major Stafford told him the story in all its gory detail, they shared a joke or two, before it was time for Troy to leave. As Troy was opening the door, Major Stafford said to him, 'Sergeant Robson.'

'Yes, sir?'

'Where do you want those vehicles?'

ACKNOWLEDGEMENTS

This book wouldn't have been possible without my literary agent David Riding at MBA; Sam Graham and the rest of the amazing team at my management agency, Red Monkey Collective; my editor Matt Phillips and his always encouraging and super-energetic team at Blink; and the creative excellence of my ghost writer Ben Dirs, who managed to put the scattered pieces of my life back together so that it made a coherent whole. Thank you all.

I should also thank the team at Minnow Productions, who bottle the magic and translate it to the screen in delivering *SAS: Who Dares Wins* to the public. It's a wonderful show and the stage for my ideas that I craved. Huge thanks also to Foxy, Billy and Ant, who typify the essence of the Special Forces and always 'pull it out of the bag' at the 11th hour: Who Dares Grins...; to Dan and Efrem, my team at StrongMen – let's make this happen; and to my team at Break-Point, who never fail to deliver, regardless of the challenges.

I take comfort from the thought that my journey has affected people in a positive way. But it has also affected some people negatively. I can only hope that anyone mentioned in this book – and anyone not – has found happiness, as I have done, and can appreciate that people come into our lives for a reason.

This project has allowed me to reflect in depth about my evolution, from that boisterous kid who couldn't stay out of trouble to the fulfilled man I am today. My family, who I love very much, know my journey better than anyone. As such, I would like to say a big thank you to my brothers Justin and Mark and sister Ashley, who make me feel so very loved. You have always opened your arms for me when I needed it, and your smiles and laughter will forever be at the forefront of my memories. Mum and Dad, thank you for the values you instilled in me when I was growing up, which continue to shape the person I am today. Last, but certainly not least, thank you Luke. I see so much of myself in you, which can be scary. But it also makes me extremely proud.

I owe an enormous debt of gratitude to Neil Foster, who was so generous with his support and empathy when I was out of control and off the rails; to Bagsy Baker, whose wise words at exactly the right time convinced an uncertain kid that he had what it took to join the most exclusive club in the world; and to Troy Robson, for the endless support, brotherhood and laughter.

My beautiful partner Laura was instrumental in my transition from a man living in a tent with nothing but optimism and a host of bright ideas to the contended person I am today. She is my rose and my rock and always shines on the cloudiest days. Laura, I will never be able to thank you enough.

I couldn't sign off without paying tribute to every man and woman who has signed on the dotted line for Queen and country, particularly those Special Forces soldiers who did such demanding work for the security of our great nation. It was these brothers I served alongside who often made the hardest challenges seem effortless. Be proud for who you are and what you stand for.

To all the above, you have gone above and beyond Break Point.